FIRST EDITION

OFFICIAL GUIDE TO

SILVER

& SILVERPLATE

by
HAL. L. COHEN

Author of
Official Guide to
Popular Antiques & Curios

Official Guide to
Paper Americana

Official Guide to
Bottles Old & New

HOUSE OF COLLECTIBLES, INC.
17 Park Avenue
New York, N.Y. 10016

ISBN: 87637-328-7

Library of Congress Number—73-93244

TABLE
OF
CONTENTS

ACKNOWLEDGEMENTS

Any book as complex and comprehensive as this one requires the help and cooperation, and contributions of many individuals, organizations, and institutions.

The help given to me in this enterprise by others associated with American Silver & Silverplate has enriched both the contents of this book, and my own experiences.

With much thanks and appreciation to the following for help in obtaining pictures and information:

MRS. DOROTHY T. RAINWATER
Our warmest thanks to Mrs. Dorothy T. Rainwater for her very generous and gracious permission to use many pictures from her new book: "AMERICAN SILVERPLATE," co-authored by H. Ivan Rainwater, and jointly published by Thomas Nelson Inc., & Everbodys' Press, Hanover, Penn. This book is the finest available on the subject of all aspects of American Silverplate, and is recommended without reservation. It is available at a cost of $15.00 from your book dealer or from the publisher.

Other books by Mrs. Rainwater on the subject of Silver & Silverplate are: AMERICAN SILVER MANUFACTURERS, and AMERICAN SPOONS, SOUVENIR & HISTORICAL, published by Everybody's Press, Hanover, Penn.

MR. E. P. HOGAN, INTERNATIONAL SILVER CO. (INSILCO)
Very special thanks to Mr. E. P. Hogan, Historical Research Librarian for the International Silver Company (INSILCO), for much time, help, and courtesy in the use of the library, files, photographs, etc., and for many prints of existing photographs.

MR. BURR SEBRING, MR. LUCIEN SERMON,
MR. W. DAN LEMESHKA,—GORHAM SILVER COMPANY.
Special acknowledgement and thanks to the various individuals at Gorham Silver for the use of the library, catalogue and photo file, and for many beautiful photographs.

VICTORIA & ALBERT MUSEUM, LONDON, ENGLAND
Many thanks to the Photo Department of this fascinating, treasure house of English, European, and American antiques and artifacts, for photos and information on Silver & Silverplate.

FLASHBACK ANTIQUES — MR. RAYMOND M. SASSON
489 Third Avenue, NYC 10016
For much help and information on Silver & Silverplate. For permission to photograph many of the beautiful Silver items in the collection.

ACKNOWLEDGEMENTS

S. H. FEINGOLD ANTIQUES — MR. STAN H. FEINGOLD
577 2nd Avenue, NYC 10016
For help and information on Silver & Silverplate collecting and pricing.
For permission to photograph Silver items in color from the collection.

To Kathy Goldwire for help in preparation and research, much thanks and appreciation.

Thanks also to ADSCO Co., Pat Sheenan, and Barbara for production and typing.
To Jonathan Stienhoff for Editorial help & creative writing.
To "Cookie" Baer for Editorial help & creative writing.

ALSO: THE METROPOLITAN MUSEUM OF ART, THE MUSEUM OF THE CITY OF NEW YORK, SAMUEL KIRK & SON SILVERSMITHS, REED & BARTON, LOU YOUNG—DEN OF ANTIQUITY, RONELLE & DAVID MIGDEN—OLD HORIZONS ANTIQUES, ETC.

If any names are omitted, it is through oversight, not intent.

PICTURE CREDITS

Listed below is the location of items and pictorial materials, and owners, used in this book.

All black & white photos credited to INSILCO were taken by Richard Croteau.
All color photos were taken by Jay Krugman—Jay Studios NYC.
INSILCO—International Silver Company, Meriden, Connecticut.

Victoria, Albert Museum—London, England: 60-74

Gorham Mfg. Co.: 77, 81-3, 87, 98, 101, 102, 103, 110, 115, 117, 139, 141, 145, 147, 148, 166, 169, 173, 175, 179, 180, 183, 184, 185, 201, 242, 243, 245, 246, 256, 258, 259, 260.

Dorothy T. Rainwater: 95, 97, 138, 189, 193, 203, 243. (Many of the pictures contributed by GORHAM & INSILCO were also contributed by Dorothy T. Rainwater.)

Insilco: 84, 85, 86, 89, 90, 91, 97, 104, 105, 111, 142, 143, 144, 171, 194, 195, 196, 197, 198, 204, 205, 206, 207, 210, 211, 217, 218, 219, 221, 222, 223-227, 228, 233, 234, 236, 244, 249, 250-55, 256, 257, 258.

1888 Catalog: 94, 96, 97, 100, 109, 116, 137, 138, 140, 146, 149, 153, 155, 159, 160, 161, 165, 167, 168, 169, 170, 174, 177, 190, 191, 195, 200, 202, 208, 209, 212, 220, 224, 225, 226, 229-32, 235, 237, 238-41, 250, 254, 258, 261, 262.

1898 Catalog: 76, 83, 87, 88, 92, 93, 94, 95, 106, 107, 118, 119, 121, 122, 123, 156, 158, 162, 164, 172, 182, 247.

Unger Bros. 1904 Catalog: 87, 145, 149, 151, 152, 154, 157, 183, 188, 192.

Flashback Antiques: 187, 199, 215.

S. H. Feingold Antiques: Color pages.

INTRODUCTION

The interest in and the collecting of American silver, sterling, coin and silverplate is growing by leaps and bounds on the part of museums, dealers, private collectors, and the general public.

The pieces representing the Victorian era (1840-1900), and Edwardian (1901-1910), were scorned and ignored in the past. With the upsurge of interest, the collecting, and buying and selling of items of this period, including Art Nouveau (1890-1910), has increased nationwide.

It is fortunate for the collector and dealer that silverplated items were not considered worth the time, expense, and trouble to melt down for their metal content; therefore, most of them escaped the lamentable fate of many examples of American sterling silver and coin silver items of the Nineteenth Century that were consigned to the melting pot for the value of the silver from which they were made.

As the auction prices of good American hallmarked pieces of Colonial, Revolutionary War, and pre-1800's skyrocketed above the $10,000 mark, the value of 1800-1861 silver showed a concurrent rise. The prospect of the average collector, dealer, or private individual obtaining a piece made by a silversmith of the pre-1800's, or pre-Civil War (1800-1861), must be considered remote at best. Therefore, this book, which is directed at this audience concerns itself with the silver and silverplate of 1865-1920, many examples of which are still readily available at antique shops, auctions, and flea markets.

A person collecting silver today has a wide selection of silver art objects from which to choose. There is also a wide selection of price ranges, so that even a person of very average means will find that there are many sterling silver and silverplated items within his reach.

This book is guide and an indicator to the Current Retail Prices of silver and silverplate of the post Civil War era 1865-1920, and to help you know the products and makers of this period. The prices quoted are approximate current Retail Prices for items in good to fine condition. Keep in mind that silver and silverplate served in a functional capacity in most households, and as such, despite care and polishing, inevitably will be in a "used" condition. Museum quality pieces kept in locked cabinets are not the province of this book.

Learn all you can about design, construction, shape, hallmarks, makers, metals, etc. Learn to appreciate the products of American Arts and Artifacts, and if you buy, buy what you like, what appeals to you, what you want to live with, and with the help of this book, knowledgeably, so you will have the double pleasure of living with beauty and investing wisely.

HISTORY OF SILVER

Silver is extremely popular among collectors, which continues the ancient tradition of investment in a precious metal, craftsmanship, and the natural beauty of a noble metal. In fact, silver has been inscribed for special occasions or used to commemorate important events, thus recording history.

Gold and silver were made frequent use of by the Egyptians, Assyrians, Phoenicians, Greeks, and Romans, and mention of gold and silver can be found on the pages of the early historical books of the Bible.

Silver has for a long time been made into utensils dedicated to the service of religion, and the more expensive articles of household decoration and use, too, have been made of silver.

During the Middle Ages & Renaissance times silver was mined predominantly in Hungary, Transylvania, and Spain. However, since the discovery of the New World, enormous quantities have been mined in Peru and Mexico. Large quantities can also be found in sea water, future oceanographic technology may make this source available.

Although silver is not as malleable as gold, it can be beaten into leaves that are a mere 1/100,000 of an inch thick. It can also be drawn into a wire that is finer even than human hair. Silver is particularly appreciated for its ability to take a brilliant polish.

Electroplated ware made during and after 1840 is called plated silver or silverplate. Plated silver is made by chemically depositing silver on a metal base. Its value depends on the depth of the plate and the taste and execution of the design.

Silver pieces made in England contain a very complex hallmark of symbols to signify the maker, his town, his date, and the silver content. Usually, silver pieces made in the U.S. are marked differently, with a simple maker's mark, although some American makers mark their work in the same manner as the English.

Pieces of silver were at one time an indication of wealth, both as symbols and in a tangible form. Before savings banks existed, people would take their silver coins to a silversmith and have them converted into usable and decorative objects. Silver, then, was an investment, with the early silversmiths playing a role not unlike that of a banker.

HISTORY OF SILVER

In colonial America, silversmiths were often prominent members of their community, Paul Revere being a notable example. Many of them, having been trained by a long apprenticeship, were highly skilled.

Since the earliest times, silver, with its natural beauty, has been devoted to the service of splendor. A precious white metal, silver lends itself excellently to the designs of the artist and craftsman, which has helped to make it one of the best known of the noble metals.

CARE OF SILVER

There are liquid preparations which are made to remove tarnish, into which silver may be dipped or polished. The original sheen on new silver can be preserved by lacquering, although when used to prevent tarnish on old silver the lacquering destroys the silver's patina. If silver is kept in a closed cabinet in which there is a piece of gum camphor (purchased at a drug store) it will stay bright long.

There are two schools of thought on the subject of replating worn silverplate. One group contends the piece should be left "as found," the other believes that since plating was, and is, a chemical process on the surface only, no change is caused by replating. We subscribe to this view and believe that replating enhances any worn piece and creates no change in originality.

HISTORY—SHEFFIELD PLATE

Sheffield was produced for a period of less than one hundred years; so that *real* Sheffield plate is actually quite rare and should not be spurned by collectors. The process of Sheffield plating was discovered in 1743 when Thomas Boulsover of Sheffield, England accidentally fused silver and copper. When the two metals were flattened into sheets, they could be handled like solid silver. This method proved good for producing small objects like buttons and buckles. But it wasn't until Joseph Hancock, Boulsover's brother-in-law and apprentice, introduced a way of plating both sides of the base metal with silver that it became possible to make silverware for the table, and large rococo objects were produced for the first time. Because of the greatly reduced cost of making Sheffield plate and the fact that it was not heavily taxed as was solid silver, people of lesser means were able to grace their homes with silver wares.

The term *plate* can be confusing. English solid silver was called plate until Sheffield rolled silver was discovered and also became known as plate. Unsuccessful attempts were made to have marks on plate clearly distinguishable from sterling silver. All this caused a controversy that raged for more than twenty-five years, until 1784. At that time, a set of standards were established which permitted Sheffield to be marked. Before 1784, all marking of Sheffield was prohibited by Parliament. Even the Goldsmiths of London were finally forced to recognize and accept the fine work being done in Sheffield plate by excellent artisans. Another confusion that arises concerning "plate" is that many eighteenth-century Sheffield pieces were reproduced in the nineteenth century. These later objects reflected not only less attention to detail, but were made by another process called electroplating.

No date marks are found on Sheffield. The craftsmen of Sheffield plate marked their articles with their initials from 1750 to 1784 when they were permitted by law to use an emblem with their names. By the early nineteenth century, the emblem can be found alone. Until it was forbidden in 1896, the mark of the crown was frequently used to indicate quality.

The manufacture of Sheffield plate ended in 1838 as abruptly as it began when the process of electroplating was introduced. Ninety years after the discovery of fusion, a great industry was dead.

WHAT IS STERLING SILVER?

In order to give silver the required degree of hardness, an alloy must be added. This alloy is usually copper, which can be added to silver without materially affecting its colors. There are 925 parts of silver and 75 parts of copper to every 1000 parts of sterling silver.

Sterling was first stamped onto silver in 1850. Most pieces of silver which were made before 1850 are of "coin" quality.

COIN PURE COIN
STANDARD DOLLAR

Marks used on Silver Products prior to 1850

STANDARDS OF STERLING SILVER

Even before the enactment of laws regarding the quality of silver products, most manufacturers had adopted the standard of not less than 900/1000, raised to 925/1000 fine. When the Gorham Company switched to the English standard, after 1868, others followed their lead.

When plated silver production first began, some manufacturers either ignored indicating the quality or marked their products "Triple" or "Quadruple" plate.

WHAT IS SILVERPLATE?

In the wake of the demise of the Sheffield plate industry, a new method of plating appeared on the scene in 1847. It was in this year that the enterprising Rogers Bros. of Hartford, Connecticut, using a process originally invented in England, began mass-producing plated silver articles by the galvano-electric method. Unlike the Sheffield fused (emalgamated) plate, this new process coated a thin layer of silver over a base metal. The base metal has changed over the years—at first Britannia (a form of pewter) was used, then nickel silver; while today mostly copper and some brass are used.

The most prolific period for electroplating occurred between 1880 and 1940. While it is still being manufactured, the quality of contemporary work falls short of the early products. Large electroplating companies are easy to identify, but this is not so of the countless small firms. Then, too, a manufacturer often marketed his house brands under different labels for competing retailers. Also, Canadian electroplate was marked U.S.A. because it was sold in America.

HOW TO IDENTIFY TYPES
OF SILVERPLATE

To identify the various types of plating combinations the items manufactured were stamped with letters that indicated the metal and the process. Prices marked as follows:

MARK	METAL COMBINATION
EPNS	Electroplate on Nickel Silver
EPBM	Electroplate on Brittania Metal
EPWM	Electroplate on White Metal
EPC	Electroplate on Copper

Three or more numbers in series stamped on a piece are manufacturers' catalog numbers.

STANDARDS OF SILVERPLATE QUALITY

*Below is reprinted a guide that appeared in the JEWELERS'
CIRCULAR MAGAZINE in 1896. This is a guide to the silver quality
of all plated ware produced in the United States. These numbers, and
figures, are to be found stamped on the bottom of silverplated items
made from 1870 to 1920.*

From: Jewelers' Circular Magazine, 1896.

SILVER PLATED WARE

Note: Manufacturers of silver plated flatware, in addition to their
trademark, stamp the quality upon their goods, almost all of them adopt-
ing the same signs and figures. These quality signs and figures are
as follows:

A.I	...........................represents standard plate.
XII	..........................represents sectional plate.
4	................represents double plate, tea spoons.
6	............................represents double plate, dessert spoons and forks.
8	..............represents double plate, table spoons.
6	..................represents triple plate, tea spoons.
9	............................represents triple plate, dessert spoons and forks.
12	................represents triple plate, table spoons.

ENGLISH & EUROPEAN SILVERPLATE MARKS

The marks shown in this table should not be confused with English & European single
figure marks. To make this distinction, check the trademark (hallmark), to determine
if the piece is American.

Another determining factor is the English and Europeans marked the number on different
parts of the same piece. A teapot for example would be marked on the body, the spout,
and the handle. An American made teapot would have the number only on the base
of the pot itself.

Another mark encountered on silverplate items of English production was the letters
"RD", followed by a number varying from 1 to 1,000,000. This was a registry mark
on electroplate as a protection against design infringement that was initiated in 1884.

TESTING FOR SILVER AND
OTHER METALS

You can tell the difference between silver and silver-substitute metals. The way of determining the percentage of silver in an object made from some kind of silver alloy is shown in the chart below.

The standard testing solution is made of 1 ounce of potassium bichromate, 6 ounces of pure nitric acid, and 2 ounces of water. In an inconspicuous spot, place a drop of the solution. As it reacts with the metal, the liquid will change color. Wash off with cold water, and a stain that identifies the metal will remain. The table below shows the results when the solution is applied to various metals. Most drug stores or chemical supply houses can supply these ingredients.

TO TEST FOR SILVER

A test solution made of:

Potassium bichromate —   1 ounce
Pure nitric acid —   6 ounces
Water —   2 ounces

Will give this reaction on the surface of the metal tested:

A. (Metal)	B. (One minute color change of liquid)	C. (Color of mark on metal)
Pure silver	Bright blood-red	Grayish white
.925 silver	Dark red	Light brown (grayish)
.800	Chocolate	Dark brown (grayish)
.500	Green	Dark brown
German Silver	Dark blue	Light gray
Nickel	Turquoise blue	Hardly any
Copper	Very dark blue	Cleaned copper
Brass	Dark brown	Light brown
Lead	Nut brown	Leaden
Tin	Reddish brown	Dark
Zinc	Light chocolate	Steel gray
Aluminum	Yellow	No stain
Platinum	Van Dyke brown	No stain
Iron	Various	Black
9-carat gold	Unchanged	No stain

The color change of the liquid is shown in column B. The liquid, not the metal, undergoes a change of color during its action for the period of one minute.

Column C shows the type of stain left when the test liquid is washed off with cold water.

MARTELÉ—GORHAM SILVER COMPANY

Punch Bowl & Ladle
CIRCA 1895

About 1895, Gorham, the largest silverware concern in America, led by its president and chief designer, decided that the time was ripe for a new style of silverware.

They were well acquainted with the modern art (Art Nouveau) movement, and had watched its development. It was felt that the limit of mechanical perfection had been almost reached, and that art was being sacrificed to mechanics. The problem was to develop a line of silverware which should be essentially an art production, and to do this it was decided to educate certain of the best men in the shop along new lines.

With this idea in mind, the creation of an entirely new set of designs was started, and these designs have been unfettered by the conventions of historic styles, but at the same time they have not shown the extreme qualities of some of the examples of modern art (Art Nouveau). This is a style in which every piece is individual, and in which no piece can be absolutely duplicated, because mechanics has no part. The form is the important thing, and the decoration, far from being conventional, partakes almost wholly of naturalistic forms: waves of the sea, natural flowers, mermaids, fishes, cloud effects—almost anything can be used provided it is treated in a naturalistic manner.

It was an extremely difficult and expensive proposition to develop the workmen to the point where they were able to turn out satisfactory pieces. The artisan was given a design and a flat sheet of metal, and told to work it out by hand, with a hammer and such hand tools as were necessary for the design he saw before him.

MARTELÉ—GORHAM SILVER COMPANY

There were many failures at first, and some discouragements, and for three or four years not one single piece was put on the market; but, finally, the small corps of select men became expert at this work, and they turned out these art productions.

Where vases, bowls, and tankards were first essayed, the movement has spread, until it now includes entire dinner services, and all sorts of ornamental and decorated silver.

As has been said, from the very nature of it, it is essentially artistic. It is the work of a man's hands, unaided by machinery of any kind. The marks of the hammer are left apparent upon the surface, giving a soft misty texture, which cannot be obtained in any other way. It is costly silverware, and must always remain so, for its production requires the greatest skill and infinite and patient labor, but it cannot be doubted that for those who seek individual art productions, who want a service which cannot be duplicated, the Martelé must appeal.

Martelé
Tankard
CIRCA 1895

SILVER DEPOSIT—SILVER OVERLAY

Silver Deposit
Toilet Bottle
CIRCA 1900

Silver deposit (variously called silver overlay or silver resist) is a technique of applying silver to clear or tinted glass, pottery, porcelain, metals (most often bronze), and wood. The silver can be thinly painted on in a thin deposit or etched and engraved in a heavy deposit. When a thick deposit appears on glass, it will always have a webbed or scrolled pattern.

Pieces of silver deposit are frequently found monogrammed (however, thin silver overlay is rarely engraved), but many articles can be found with no monograms. The latter are preferred by dealers; however, the collector, not so concerned with resale, might enjoy the sentiment behind the initials, as they probably indicate the object was given as a treasured gift.

There was a technique that was used to give the effect of a heavy silver deposit. Here, the glass was produced with raised scrolls and webs and a thin layer of silver was painted on these raised areas. This pseudo type of silver deposit, however, is easily discernable.

In 1893 a very beautiful technique was introduced that was executed by covering the entire surface of an object with a thin layer of silver, then one of gold, and finally another of silver. A layer of resist varnish was then applied and the unwanted areas were etched out. The etching resulted in a handsome design of silver and gold.

SILVER DEPOSIT—SILVER OVERLAY

Martelé
Silver Deposit
Ewer

Silver deposit first appeared in the 1880's and had its heyday during a thirty-year period from the 1890's to the end of the First World War. While articles had previously been mounted with silver, it was not until electricity was invented that silver deposit—the fusion of silver to other types of materials—was possible. Many processes to carry out the technique of silver deposit were patented and a collector would do well to acquaint himself with them.

Silver deposit is still being produced; however, one can detect the old from the new deposit because the old pieces tarnish while the new pieces are coated with rhodium to prevent it. The oxidation that occurs when an object tarnishes creates exciting, contrasting effects when the surface areas of the old, heavy pieces are polished to a sheen and the recessed areas are left oxidized.

HISTORY OF "ROGERS BROS.—1847"
AND THE INTERNATIONAL SILVER COMPANY

World renowned for its fine tableware, the history of The International Silver Company, and its predecessors, is a history of America's silversmithing.

Early records go back to 1808 when Ashbil Griswold, having learned his trade from the famous Danforth family, set up his pewter shop in Meriden, Connecticut.

Soon he expanded his business to include britannia ware, and, around the middle of the 19th century he joined other independent makers of pewter and britannia ware to finance the Yankee Peddlers . . . . resourceful men who traveled about selling and bartering. Meriden became known as the center for pewter, britannia ware and coin silver. Even today it is known as "THE SILVER CITY."

Then in 1852, Griswold's associates and successors, headed by Horace C. Wilcox, formed the Meriden Britannia Company—a move that united independent manufacturers and put into force better selling and business methods. Meriden Britannia Company was the leading spirit and direct forerunner of The International Silver Company.

The saga of International would not be complete without reference to the Rogers Brothers who developed the electroplating process in 1847. This brought handsome silver economically to the tables of thousands of homes in America. The Rogers Brothers became affiliated with the Meriden Britannia Company in 1862 thus uniting two famous groups of silversmiths. Since this date, "1847 ROGERS BROS." has been one of the most famous International tableware trademarks.

The Company was incorporated in 1898 by a number of independent New England silversmiths whose family backgrounds date back to the days the Pilgrims first set foot on American soil. Through the years, International has developed steadily to become the largest silverware manufacturer in the world.

The home office of the Company is in Meriden, and its silverware products are manufactured in five different plants, two of them in Meriden, two in Wallingford, and one in Perth, Ontario, Canada.

HISTORY OF ROGERS BROS.—1847
AND THE INTERNATIONAL SILVER COMPANY

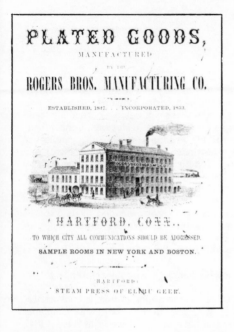

1860 ROGERS
BROS.
CATALOG

EARLY
ROGERS
BROS. AD

THE ROGERS BROS.

HALLMARKS—ROGERS BROS. & INTERNATIONAL SILVER ASSOCIATES

WHITE METAL

NICKEL SILVER

STERLING

21

HALLMARKS—ROGERS BROS. & INTERNATIONAL SILVER ASSOCIATES

MADE AND
GUARANTEED BY

••• ROGERS BROS.

Pewter
by
Wilcox

STERLING

URITAN PEWTER

Old Colony Pewter

HALLMARKS—ROGERS BROS. &
INTERNATIONAL SILVER ASSOCIATES

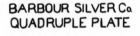

HALLMARKS—ROGERS BROS. & INTERNATIONAL SILVER ASSOCIATES

1847 Rogers Bros. ⊕ XII ᵀᴿⁱᴾˡᴱ

🗡 ROGERS & HAMILTON, A 1."

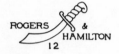

ROGERS & HAMILTON 12

INLAID

HESCO

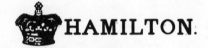

HAMILTON.

AMERICAN SILVER CO.

AMERICAN SILVER PLATE CO.

A. S. CO.   1857

1857 "STANDARD OF THE WORLD"

HOLMES & TUTTLE

H. & T. MFG. CO.

INSICO STAINLESS

"WORLD BRAND"

⚓ W. R.& S.

VIANDE

X S TRIPLE

OLD COMPANY PLATE

ROGERS CUTLERY CO.

M S C W

Ⓦ W. M.CO. Ⓦ

ROGERS CO

⊕ HOLMES & EDWARDS XIV

E HOLMES & EDWARDS STERLING INLAID HE

E HOLMES & EDWARDS SILVER - INLAID HE

Ⓔ STERLING INLAID

HE

XIV

HOLMES H EDWARDS

SUPER-PLATE

STRATFORD SILVER PLATE CO.

STRATFORD SILVER CO.

STRATFORD PLATE

STRATFORD SILVER CO AXI

INTERNATIONAL SILVER CO.

INTERNATIONAL

I.S. CO.

INSICO

R. & B.

R.C. CO.

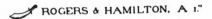

24

HALLMARKS—ROGERS BROS. & INTERNATIONAL SILVER ASSOCIATES

1847 ROGERS BROS.

WM. ROGERS & SON ⚓ ROGERS ⚓ WM. ROGERS MFG. CO.

1865 WM. ROGERS MFG. CO. ★ ROGERS & BRO.

🐾 Wm Rogers ★

HOLMES&EDWARDS
INLAID

INTERNATIONAL SILVER COMPANY

INTERNATIONAL S. CO.

STRATFORD SILVERPLATE

SILCO STAINLESS

I.S.CO.

VICTOR S. CO.

SERVICE PLATE

AMERICAN SILVER CO.

MANOR PLATE

R. C. CO. AI PLUS

 INTERNATIONAL SILVER COMPANY

AMERICAN HALLMARKS

By 1800 many fake hallmarks were being used in the colonies to dupe the buyer into believing he was purchasing a silver article made in England. Therefore, you must first make sure the mark on a piece of silver is American.

Frequently, only one mark was used by early colonial silversmiths, so that if an object has several hallmarks, especially four or five, it might very well be English. No official marker-date system was ever exacted in the colonies, except in Baltimore between 1814 and 1830. Thus, much early American silver is not marked at all, while those pieces that are, bear the silversmith's initials or his surname in full (in England only initials were allowed). Before the eighteenth century, these initials or names were enclosed within a heart, shield, star, square, oval, etc. Later they were usually enclosed in a simple rectangle. Some early silversmiths, following English tradition, placed a crown above their initials. Surnames with or without the initial of the given name came into use early in the nineteenth century or without the initial of the given name came into use early in the nineteenth century to prevent any confusion among the growing number of American silversmiths who frequently had similar initials. Sometimes the city or town where an article was made was also punched to assure proper identification.

Sometimes a jeweler or store owner would add his name to that of the silversmith or manufacturer, or to a piece of silver that had not been stamped at all. While this confusion and the lack of a maker-date system can make validation of an article difficult and determination of exact dates virtually impossible, approximate dates can be arrived at by knowing the years the silversmith worked, and the style and form of the object in question.

By 1830 the words *coin, pure coin, dollar, standard, premium,* or the letter *C* and *D* were placed on silver to indicate that it was 900 parts out of 1000 parts silver. By 1860 the word *sterling* was frequently used to indicate 925 parts silver.

In the 1840's large companies such as Gorham, Tiffany, and Samuel Kirk & Son began to manufacture silver ware. Retailers often added their own marks to that of the manufacturer, which is why it is difficult to determine the maker of much nineteenth-century silver.

AMERICAN SILVERSMITHS HALLMARKS

American silversmiths marks were in most cases made up of the maker's name or initials. Inside the many hallmark shapes shown, these letters or names were stamped. Pseudo hallmarks and other marks were often used. These were made to resemble the English silversmith's guild marks. In the psuedo marks, a star, a hand, a bird, or a head was often used along with the maker's mark.

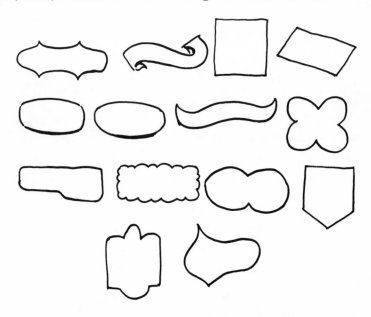

PSEUDO HALLMARKS

AMERICAN SILVERSMITHS HALLMARKS
1800-1900

On the following pages are a list of American Silversmiths from 1800-1900.

They are listed by Hallmark, Name, City and State, Date, and Shape of Hallmark. These individual Silversmiths can be matched with the illustrations of Hallmarks on pages 37 to 49, by matching the letters in the first column with the letters in the illustrated Hallmark, this will give you the complete description of the Silversmith.

Hallmark	Silversmith	City & State	Date	Type of Hallmark
AB	Abel Buel	New Haven, Conn.	1742-1825	Elongated oval punch
AC	Alexander Camman	Albany, N.Y.	Early 1800's	Oblong punch
AC	Aaron Cleveland	Norwich, Conn.	About 1820	Oblong punch-tilted corners
AC	Albert Cole	New York, N.Y.		
AD	Amos Doolittle	New Haven, Conn.	1754-1832	Oval punch
A-E-W	Andrew E. Warner	Baltimore, Md.	1786-1870	Oblong punch-serrated ends; also in plain oblong punch AEW with interlaced italic caps
A & G.W.	A. & G. Welles	Boston, Mass.	Early 1800's	Oblong punch
A.J.&Co.	A. Jacobs & Co.	Philadelphia, Pa.	Circa, 1820	Oblong punch
BB	Benjamin Bussey	Dedham, Mass.	1757-1842	Oblong punch
BB	Benjamin Benjamin	New York, N.Y.	Circa, 1825	Oblong punch-tilted corners, or incised
B & D	Barrington & Davenport	Philadelphia, Pa.	Circa, 1805	Oblong punch-Serrated edged
B.G.	Baldwin Gardiner	Philadelphia, Pa.	Circa, 1814	Oblong punch
B.G & Co.	B. Gardiner & Co.	New York, N.Y.	Circa, 1836	Oblong punch
B&I or B&J	Boyce & Jones	New York, N.Y.	Circa, 1825	Both in oblong punch
B & M	Bradley & Merriman	New Haven, Conn.	Circa, 1825	Shaped to include star or oblong punch
B & R	Brower & Rusher	New York, N.Y.	About 1834	Oblong punch
B T & B	Ball, Tompkins & Black	New York, N.Y.	Circa, 1839	Oblong punch
BW & Co.	Butler, Wise & Co.	Philadelphia, Pa.	About 1845	Oblong-rounded end

AMERICAN SILVERSMITHS HALLMARKS
1800-1900

Hallmark	Silversmith	City & State	Date	Type of Hallmark
CB	Clement Beecher	Berlin, Conn.	1778-1869	Oblong or rounded punch-serrated edges
CC	Christian Cornelius	Philadelphia, Pa.	About 1810	Oblong punch
CC & D	Charters, Cann & Dunn	New York, N.Y.	About 1850	Oblong punch
CC & S	Curtis, Candee & Stiles	Woodbury, Conn.	About 1840	Oblong punch
CH	Charles Hequembourg, Jr.	New Haven, Conn.	1760-1851	Shaped punch
CH	Christopher Hughes	Baltimore, Md.	1744-1824	Oblong punch
CL	Charles Leach	Boston, Mass.	1765-1814	Oblong punch-waved edges
CLB	Charles L. Boehme	Baltimore, Md.	1774-1868	Oblong punch
C&M	Coit & Mansfield	Norwich, Conn.	About 1816	Oblong punch-also with rounded ends
C&P	Cleveland & Post	Norwich, Conn.	Circa, 1815	Oblong punch-also with serrated edges
C&P	Curry & Preston	Philadelphia, Pa.	About 1831	Oblong punch
CVGF or C.V.G.F.	Collins V. G. Forbes	New York, N.Y.	About 1816	Oblong punch
C.W.	Christian Wiltberger	Philadelphia, Pa.	1770-1851	Oblong punch
D:D or DD	Daniel Dupuy	Philadelphia, Pa.	1719-1807	Oblong, shaped or oval punch
DM	David Mygatt	Danbury, Conn.	1777-1822	Oblong punch
DM	David Moseley	Boston, Mass.	1753-1812	Oblong punch
DN	David I. Northee	Salem, Mass.	d. 1788	Oblong punch
D&P	Downing & Phelps	New York, N.Y.	About 1810	Oblong punch
D.T.G.	D.T. Goodhue	Boston, Mass.	fl. 1840's	Oblong punch
D&W	Davis & Watson	Boston, Mass.	Circa, 1815	Oblong punch with italic caps
EB	Ezekial Burr	Providence, R.I.	1764-1846	EB in italic caps, shaped or oval punch-also oblong punch

AMERICAN SILVERSMITHS HALLMARKS
1800-1900

Hallmark	Silversmith	City & State	Date	Type of Hallmark
EB&CO	Erastus Barton & Co.	New York, N.Y.	fl. 1820's	Oblong punch
E-C	Elias Camp	Bridgeport, Conn.	About 1825	Oblong punch-serrated edges
EC	Ebenezer Chittenden	New Haven, Conn.	1726-1812	Oblong or oval punch
EH	Eliphaz Hart	Norwich, Conn.	1789-1866	Oblong punch
EL	Edward Lang	Salem, Mass.	1742-1830	Oblong punch
EME	Edgar M. Eoff	New York, N.Y.	1785-1858	Oblong punch
EP.	Edward Pear	Boston, Mass.	fl. 1830's	Oblong punch-serrated edges
EP	Elias Pelletreau	Southampton, N.Y.	1726-1810	Oblong punch
EPL	Edward P. Lescure	Philadelphia, Pa.	fl. 1820's	Oblong punch with italic caps
E&P	Eoff & Phyfe	New York, N.Y.	About 1844	Oblong punch, P forms round end
E&S	Easton & Sanford	Nantucket, Mass.	About 1816	Oblong punch
F.&G.	Fletcher & Gardiner	Philadelphia, Pa.	About 1812	Oblong punch
F&H	Farrington & Hunnewell	Boston, Mass.	fl. 1830's	Oblong punch
F.M.	Frederick Marquand	New York, N.Y.	fl. 1820's	Oblong punch, also F-M
F&M	Frost & Munford	Providence, R.I.	About 1810	Oblong punch-serrated edges
F.W.C.	Francis W. Cooper	New York, N.Y.	fl. 1840's	Small oblong punch with FWC over NY
GB or G.B.	Geradus Boyce	New York, N.Y.	About 1814	Oblong punch
GC	George Canon	Warwick, R.I.	Early 1800's	Oblong punch
G&D	Goodwin & Dodd	Hartford, Conn.	Circa, 1813	Oblong punch
G&H	Gale & Hayden	New York, N.Y.	fl. 1840's	Oblong punch-tilted corners
G&M	Gale & Moseley	New York, N.Y.	About 1830	Oblong punch with serrated or plain edges
GRD	G.R. Downing	New York, N.Y.	Circa, 1810	Oblong punch

AMERICAN SILVERSMITHS HALLMARKS
1800-1900

Hallmark	Silversmith	City & State	Date	Type of Hallmark
G&S	Gale & Stickler	New York, N.Y.	fl. 1820's	Oblong punch
G.W.&H	Gale, Wood & Hughes	New York, N.Y.	About 1835	Oblong punch with serrated or plain edges
H&B	Hart & Brewer	Middletown, Conn.	Early 1800's	Oblong punch
H&H	Hall & Hewson	Albany, N.Y.	About 1819	Oblong punch
H&I	Heydorn & Imlay	Hartford, Conn.	Circa, 1810	Oblong punch- waved edges
H.L	Harvey Lewis	Philadelphia, Pa.	About 1811	Oblong punch
H.L.W.&CO	Henry L. Webster & Co.	Providence, R.I.	fl. 1840's	Oblong Punch
H&M	Hall & Merriman	New Haven, Conn.	Circa, 1826	Incised
HP	Henry Pitkin	East Hartford, Conn.	Circa, 1830's	Flattened octagonal punch
HRT	Henry R. Truax	Albany, N.Y.	About 1815	Plain HRT in plain oblong punch
HS	Hezekia Silliman	New Haven, Conn.	1739-1804	Oblong punch
H&S	Hart & Smith	Baltimore, Md.	Circa, 1815	Oblong punch- also H&S incised
H&S	Hotchkiss & Shreuder	Syracuse, N.Y.	Mid 1800's	H in Diamond-shape punch & round punch, S in round punch
H&W	Hart & Wilcox	Norwich, Conn.	Early 1800's	Oblong punch
IA	I. Adam	Alexandria, Va.	Circa, 1800	Oval punch, italic caps
I-C	Joseph Carpenter	Norwich, Conn.	1747-1804	Oblong punch
I.C or IC	John Coburn	Boston, Mass.	1725-1803	Square punch
IHL	Josiah H. Lownes	Philadelphia, Pa.	Circa, 1822	JHL in oblong punch
I-I	Joseph Jennings	Norwalk, Conn.	1739-1817	Oblong punch
IK	Joseph Keeler	Norwalk, Conn.	1786-1824	Plain or serrated edges, oblong punch
IL or I-L	John Lynch	Baltimore, Md.	1761-1848	Square punch
I-P	Joseph Perkins	Newburyport, Mass.	1766-1849	Crowned IP in shaped scutcheon punch

AMERICAN SILVERSMITHS HALLMARKS
1800-1900

Hallmark	Silversmith	City & State	Date	Type of Hallmark
I.P.T. & SON	John P. Trott & Son	New London, Conn.	fl. 1820's	Oblong punch
I&PT	John & Peter Targee	New York, N.Y.	Early 1800's	Oblong punch
I-R	Joseph Rogers	Newport, R.I.	About 1808	Flattened oval punch
IR&S	Isaac Reed & Son	Stamford, Conn.	Circa, 1810	Oblong punch
IW	Joshua Weaver	West Chester, Pa.	Circa, 1815	Shaped oval punch
IWF	John W. Forbes	New York, N.Y.	About 1805	IWF over NY-oblong punch
J&A.S	J.&A. Simmons	New York, N.Y.	Early 1800's	Oblong punch
J.B	John Boyce	New York, N.Y.	Circa, 1800	Oblong punch-found with NY in separate Oblong punch
J.B	James Black	Philadelphia, Pa.	About 1811	Oblong punch
J.C.M.	John C. Moore	New York, N.Y.	fl. 1840's	Oblong punch
J.F	Foster & Richards	New York, N.Y.	About 1815	Oblong punch
J.H.C	John H. Connor	New York, N.Y.	fl. 1830's	Oblong punch
J.L.W	John L. Westervell	Newburgh, N.Y.	About 1845	Oblong punch
JM	J. Merchant	New York, N.Y.	Circa, 1860-80	Oval punch
J.P.W.	Joseph P. Warner	Baltimore, Md.	1811-1862	Oblong punch
JS	Joel Sayre	New York, N.Y.	1778-1818	Oblong punch
J.S.B	John Starr Blackman	Danbury, Conn.	1777-1851	Flattened oval or oblong punch
JW	James Ward	Hartford, Conn.	1768-1856	Oval punch
J.W.B	Joseph W. Boyd	New York, N.Y.	Circa, 1820	Oblong punch
J.W.F.	John W. Faulkner	New York, N.Y.	Circa, 1835	Oblong punch
J&W	Jones & Ward	Boston, Mass.	Mid 1800's	Oval punch
K.C.&J.	Kidney, Cann & Johnson	New York, N.Y.	Mid 1800's	Oblong punch
K&D	Kidney & Dunn	New York, N.Y.	fl. 1840's	Oblong punch-plain or serrated edges
K.&S.	Kirk & Smith	Baltimore, Md.	Circa, 1815	Oblong punch

AMERICAN SILVERSMITHS HALLMARKS
1800-1900

Hallmark	Silversmith	City & State	Date	Type of Hallmark
L.B	Luther Bradley	New Haven, Conn.	1772-1830	Oblong punch
L&G	Lincoln & Green	Boston, Mass.	Circa, 1810	Oblong punch
LH	Littleton Holland	Baltimore, Md.	1770-1847	Oblong punch-italic caps
L&W	Leonard & Wilson	Philadelphia, Pa.	About 1847	Oblong punch-serrated edges
MB	Miles Beach	Litchfield, Conn.	1743-1828	M-B in oblong punch or rounded oval punch
M&B	Merriman & Bradley	New Haven, Conn.	About 1817	Oblong punch-Plain or serrated edges
M.G or MG	Miles Gorham	New Haven, Conn.	1757-1847	Oblong punch
M.J or MJ	Munson Jarvis	Stamford, Conn.	1742-1824	Oblong punch
MM	Marcus Merriman	New Haven, Conn.	1762-1850	M-M in oblong punch-M in square punch-MM in separaet punch
M.M&Co	Marcus Merriman & Co.	New Haven, Conn.	About 1817	Oblong punch-serrated edges
MP or M-P	Matthew Petit	New York, N.Y.	About 1811	Oblong punch
N-A	Nathaniel Austin	Boston, Mass.	1734-1818	Oblong punch
NH	Nicholas Hutchins	Baltimore, Md.	1777-1845	Flattened oval punch
N.H&CO	N. Harding & Co.	Boston, Mass.	Circa, 1830	Oblong punch
NS	Nathaniel Shipman	Norwich, Conn.	1764-1853	Oblong punch
NV	Nathaniel Vernon	Charleston, S.C.	1777-1843	Oblong punch
O&S	Oakes & Spencer	Hartford, Conn.	Circa, 1814	Oblong punch
PDR	Peter De Riemer	Philadelphia, Pa.	1736-1814	Oblong punch-also with rounded ends
P.L.	Peter Lupp	New Brunswick, N.J.	1797-1827	Oval punch
P.L.K	Peter L. Krider	Philadelphia, Pa.	Mid 1800's	Oblong punch
P.M	P. Mood	Charleston, S.C.	About 1806	Oblong punch
PR	Paul Revere II	Boston, Mass.	1735-1818	PR in italic caps-circle or oblong punch

AMERICAN SILVERSMITHS HALLMARKS
1800-1900

Hallmark	Silversmith	City & State	Date	Type of Hallmark
P.S	Philip Sadtler	Baltimore, Md.	1771-1860	Shaped oblong punch
P&U	Pelletreau & Upson	New York, N.Y.	About 1818	Oblong punch
R.&A.C.	R.&A. Campbell	Baltimore, Md.	About 1853	Oblong punch
RB	Roswell Bartholomew	Hartford, Conn.	1781-1830	Oblong punch-serrated edges
RC	Robert Campbell	Baltimore, Md.	About 1834	Oblong punch
RE or R-E	Robert Evans	Boston, Mass.	1812	Oblong punch
R&G	Riggs & Griffith	Baltimore, Md.	About 1816	Oblong punch
R-M	Reuben Merriman	Litchfield, Conn.	1783-1866	Oblong punch-serrated edges
RR	Richard Riggs	Philadelphia, Pa.	1819	Shaped oval oblong punch
RW or R-W	Robert Wilson	New York, N.Y.	About 1816	Oval punch
R&WW	R.&W. Wilson	Philadelphia, Pa.	fl. 1820's	Oblong punch
SA	Samuel Avery	Preston, Conn.	1760-1836	Oblong punch-also with SA in italic caps
SB	Standish Barry	Baltimore, Md.	1763-1844	Oblong punch
SB	Samuel Buel	Middletown, Conn.	1742-1819	S-B in oblong punch-also rounded oval punch
S&B	Shepherd & Boyd	Albany, N.Y.	About 1810	Oblong punch
SC&Co	Simon Chaudrons & Co.	Philadelphia, Pa.	About 1807	Oblong punch
S&C	Storrs & Cooley	New York, N.Y.	Circa, 1830	Shaped punch
S*D	Samuel Drowne	Portsmouth, N.H.	1749-1815	Flattened oval punch
SH or S-H	Stephen Hardy	Portsmouth, N.H.	1781-1843	Oblong punch
S.K	Samuel Kirk	Baltimore, Md.	1792-1872	Oblong punch-plain or serrated edges
S-M	Samuel Merriman	New Haven, Conn.	1769-1805	Oblong punch
S&M	Sibley & Marble	New Haven, Conn.	1801-1806	Oblong punch

AMERICAN SILVERSMITHS HALLMARKS
1800-1900

Hallmark	Silversmith	City & State	Date	Type of Hallmark
S&R	Sayre & Richards	New York, N.Y.	About 1802	Flattened oval or oblong punch
SS	Silas Sawin	Boston, Mass.	About 1823	Square punch
TA	Thomas Arnold	Newport, R.I.	1739-1828	Oblong punch- Roman or italic caps
TB	Timothy Brigden	Albany, N.Y.	About 1813	Oblong punch- serrated edges
T-B	Thomas Burger	New York, N.Y.	Circa, 1805	Oblong punch
TC	Thomas Carson	Albany, N.Y.	Circa, 1815	Shaped punch
T.C.C.	Thomas Chester Coit	Norwich, Conn.	Circa, 1812	Oblong punch
T.C&H	Thomas Carson & Hall	Albany, N.Y.	About 1818	Oblong punch
T.E.	Thomas Knox Emery	Boston, Mass.	1781-1815	Oblong punch
T.E.S	T.E. Stebbins	New York, N.Y.	About 1810	Oblong punch
T&H	Taylor & Hinsdale	New York, N.Y.	About 1810	Oblong punch
T-K	Thomas Kinne	Norwich, Conn.	1786-1824	TK and T.K. in oblong punches
T.K.	Thaddeus Keeler	New York, N.Y.	About 1805	Oblong punch
TN	Thomas Norton	Farmington, Conn.	1796-1806	Oblong punch
T.W	Thomas H. Warner	Baltimore, Md.	1780-1828	Shaped oval punch
T-W	Thomas Whartenby	Philadelphia, Pa.	About 1811	Oblong punch
U&B	Ufford & Burdick	New Haven, Conn.	Circa, 1814	Oblong punch
V&W	VanNess & Waterman	New York, N.Y.	About 1835	Oblong punch
W&B	Ward & Bartholomew	Hartford, Conn.	About 1804	Oblong punch
W.B.N.	William B. North	New York, N.Y.	1787-1838	Oblong punch
W&B	Ward & Bartholomew	Hartford, Conn.	About 1804	Oblong punch- plain or serrated edges

AMERICAN SILVERSMITHS HALLMARKS
1800-1900

Hallmark	Silversmith	City & State	Date	Type of Hallmark
W-C	William Cleveland	New London, Conn.	1770-1837	WC in oblong punch-
W-F	William Forbes	New York, N.Y.	About 1830	Oblong punch
WG	William Gale	New York, N.Y.	About 1816	Oblong punch
W.G.	William Gurley	Norwich, Conn.	Early 1800's	Oblong punch
W&G	Woodward & Grosjean	Boston, Mass.	About 1847	Oblong punch-rounded ends
W.G&S	William Gale & Son	New York, N.Y.	About 1823	Oblong punch
W.H.	William Homes, Jr.	New York, N.Y.	1742-1835	Oblong punch-also WH
W&H	Wood & Hughes	New York, N.Y.	About 1846	Oblong punch
WJ	William B. Johonnot	Middletown, Conn.	1766-1849	Oblong punch
WM	William Moulton	Newburyport, Mass.	Circa, 1807	Oblong punch
W-R	William Roe	Kingston, N.Y.	Early 1800's	Oblong punch
W-S	William Simes	Portsmouth, N.H.	1773-1824	Oblong punch-rounded corners
W-S-N	William S. Nichol	Newport, R.I.	1785-1871	Oblong punch
W.S.P. with TR	Pelletreau & Richards	New York, N.Y.	Circa, 1825	Separate oblong punches
W.S.P.	William Smith Pelletreau	Southampton, L.I., N.Y.	1786-1842	Oblong punch-serrated edges
W.W.	William Ward	Litchfield, Conn.	1742-1828	Oblong punch
WWG	W.W. Gaskins	Providence, R.I.	1830's	Oblong punch
ZS	Zebulon Smith	Maine	1786-1865	

AMERICAN SILVERSMITHS HALLMARKS
1830 - 1900

ACKNOWLEDGEMENT

On the following pages are illustrated a cross-section of American Silversmiths Hallmarks of the period, 1830-1910, they are used with the kind permission of MR. MALCOLM ROGERS, PRESIDENT OF CRACKER BARREL PRESS, SOUTHHAMPTON, NEW YORK, and are taken with permission, from **"AMERICAN SILVERSMITHS AND THEIR MARKS"** (Second Edition), by STEPHEN G. ENSKO, the most complete and accurate book on American Silversmiths Hallmarks from 1650-1850, this book has much other information on Silver and Silversmiths.

This book is highly recommended and is available from the Publisher:

CRACKER BARREL PRESS
P.O. BOX 1287
SOUTHAMPTON, L.I., N.Y. 11968

at a cost of $2.00 postpaid.

Other books on American Antiques are published by CRACKER BARREL PRESS.

HALLMARKS 1830-1900

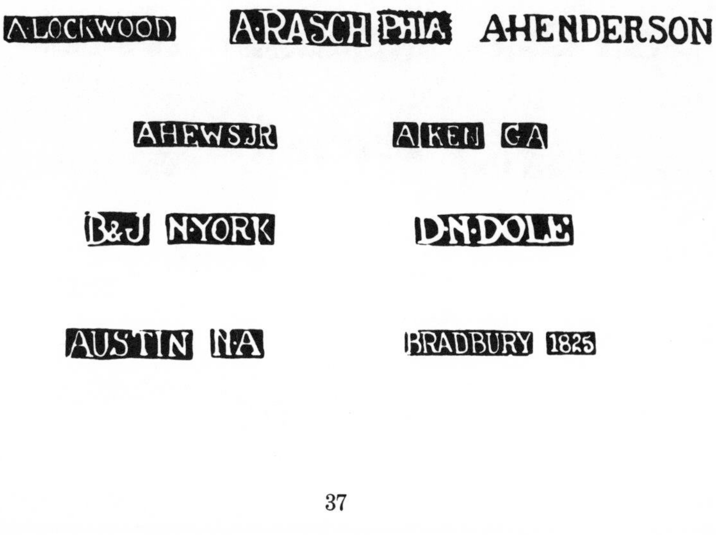

A·LOCKWOOD   A·RASCH PHA   AHENDERSON

AHEWS.JR   AIKEN GA

B&J N·YORK   D·N·DOLE

AUSTIN NA   BRADBURY 1825

AB BUEL   ARNOLD JA TA

A HENDERSON

A Beach
                                        A.SANBORN LOWELL

                        AHEWSJR

AC ACLEVELAND   A HOLMES   A.STOWELL JR

                        AIKEN GA

                                        A.T.BATTELS

                A JOHNSTON STER

AC BENEDICT 28 BOWERY   A WHITE

A CUTLER BOSTON   A.L.Lincoln   A WILLARD

HGW AEW   AOSTHOFF   ℙ STERLING

AE WARNER 11²   APPLETON   A&W-WOOD

                            Babcock
                                    BACHMAN

A C WARNER   🜨 STERLING

                                    BAILEY & KITCHEN
A.G STORM   A.RASCH & CO

AMERICAN SILVERSMITHS HALLMARKS
1830-1900

BALDWIN & CO   NEWARK

BALL BLACK & CO

BALL TOMPKINS & BLACK

BARD & LAMONT

Barry   BARRY   No 92

BB

BB   B BENJAMIN

BLEASOM & REED.

B.M.BAILEY   LUDLOW

B & M   B&M

BOSWORTH

BOYCE & JONES

BRADY

BROWN & KIRBY

BRYAN

B & R

BT & B

BUEL

BW & CO

C Boehm

CAPELLE   ST.LOUIS

CB   CB

C BARD   205 ARCH ST

C BILLON

C BREWER

CC & D

C.C. & S.

CD SULLIVAN

CH   C HEQUEMBOURG

CH   CH

CH.PHELPS

CHURCH & ROGERS

C & I.W. FORBES

C & J WARNER

CLARK   NORWALK

CLARK & BRO.

CL.B   STERLING

Cl. Boehm

AMERICAN SILVERSMITHS HALLMARKS
1830-1900

CLEVELAND WC

C.Wittberger

C.Wittberger

C.WESTPHAL

WKC

COE & UPTON NY

C.W.STEWART LEX.KT.

COOPER & FISHER
131 AMITY ST. NY.

COWLES

C.Wynn

DAVID KINSEY

Currier & Trott

D.ARROW

DAVIS.PALMER & CO

CURRY & PRESTON

D.B.Thompson

D.B.Thompson

CURTISS·CANDEE & STILES

D.B.MILLER

CURTISS & DUNNING

De Larue

D.GODDARD & SON

CURTISS & STILES

DKINSEY

D.M.FITCH

CURTISS & STILES

DM DMYGATT

DUHME

C·W

D.SULLIVAN & CO.

C.Warner

PURE SILVER COIN

D.T.G

D.T.GOODHUE

AMERICAN SILVERSMITHS HALLMARKS
1830-1900

EASTON & SANFORD

E.ADRIANCE

EB EB EB E.BURR

E.BENJAMIN

E.BENJAMIN & CO.

E.BORHEK STANDARD

E.BRADY

E.BURR E.BURR E.Burr

E.C.

E.COIT PURE COIN

E.CUTLER

E.DAVIS E.Davis

E.&D.KINSEY

E.&D.KINSEY

EH E.HART

E.HART EH

EL LANG

E.Lincoln

E.M.E

E.MEAD

EOLLES & DAY HARTFORD

E.P.

E.Stillman

E&S

E.Whiton

FELLOWS & STORM

FESSENDEN

F&H

F.LOCKWOOD

FOSTER

FORBES & SON

FORBES & SON

FROBISHER

F.S.BLACKMAN

F.S.B&Co. DANBURY

F.S.Sandford

F.W.C NY

F.W.COOPER . 900/1000

G.AIKEN

GALE & WILLIS

AMERICAN SILVERSMITHS HALLMARKS
1830-1900

G.BAKER G.M.ZAHM G.W.BULL G.W.&H

G.B.BOTSFORD G&M G&M G.W.&N.C.PLATT

G.C.CLARK GOODING H.A.McMASTER

GELSTON Gorham & Thurber HARDY

GELSTON LADD & CO NY HIGBIE & CROSBY

G.EOFF G.EOFF Gorham & Webster H&M

GEO.W.WEBB GOULD & WARD

G.GRAY H.L.WEBSTER

GREGG HAYDEN & CO H.McKEEN

G&H GRIFFEN & HOYT

GIBSON GRIFFEN & HOYT HOBBS

GILL G.S.GELSTON H.L.W.&CO Providence RI

G.LOOMIS&CO ERIE G.TERRY HOSFORD

AMERICAN SILVERSMITHS HALLMARKS
1830-1900

HOOD&TOBEY   I·M·MULLIN   I.M   ❖   ĬP

ĬHP

I·MUNROE   I·P   J·PERKINS

H.PORTER&CO

I.PT&SON   I.SPorter   I.N.TOY

H.SADD

JABBOTT

JACCARD&CO

H ❖ S ❖   HUTTON ❖ ALBANY   J.B.JONES   J·B·JONES

Jas·Thomson   J.B.M FADDEN

I.BROCK   NEW·YORK   J.C.M   J.CONNING MOBILE

I.FOSTER FOSTER   J.CURRY J   PHILA

IHL JHL   J.DECKER

H IL H·YNCH ❖   J.D.MASON   J.FITCH ❖

I.McMullin   J.McMullin   ❖   JEFFREY R.BRACKET

J.J.LOW&CO   J.P.W   J.SARGEANT   HARTFORD

J.KEDZIE 🐦 Ⓡ 🖐   J.S.B J.S.B   J.S.SHARRARD

J.L.MOORE J.L.Moore

J.LORD J.LORD   J.T.RICE   Albany

J.L.W   JW   J.WARD HARTFORD   J.WALTER

J.LYNCH   J.WARD   HARTFORD

J.WATSON

J.MEREDITH

J.W.BEEBE   🔷 J&W 🔷

.JOHN B.AKIN DANVILLE   J.W.BEEBE&CO   K.C.&J.

JOHN BIGELOW PURE COIN   J.WEBB   K&D K&D

J.W.F.   Kirk KIRK SK H

JOHN H.TYLER&CO   J.W.FAULKNER   371 Pearl St.

JONES.BALL&POOR   LANG EL   LANGE

JONES.LOWS&BALL   L.B   LEONARD

Joseph J.Rice   £H 🐦 STERLIN

AMERICAN SILVERSMITHS HALLMARKS
1830-1900

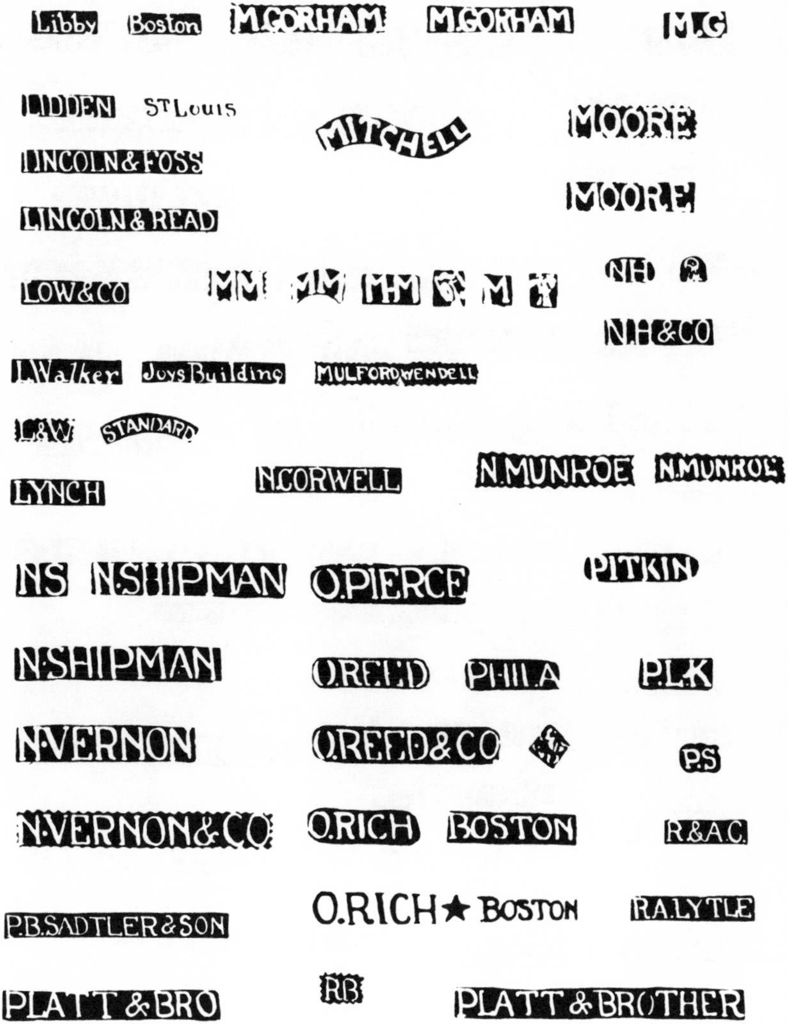
Libby
Boston
M.GORHAM
M.GORHAM
M.G
LIDDEN
ST Louis
MITCHELL
MOORE
LINCOLN & FOSS
MOORE
LINCOLN & READ
LOW & CO
MM
MM
M.M
M
NH
NH & CO
L.Walker
Joys Building
MULFORD WENDELL
L&W
STANDARD
LYNCH
N.CORWELL
N.MUNROE
N.MUNROE
NS
N.SHIPMAN
O.PIERCE
PITKIN
N.SHIPMAN
O.REED
PHILA
P.L.K
N.VERNON
O.REED & CO
P.S
N.VERNON & CO
O.RICH
BOSTON
R & A.C.
O.RICH ★ BOSTON
R.A.LYTLE
P.B.SADTLER & SON
R.B
PLATT & BRO
PLATT & BROTHER

AMERICAN SILVERSMITHS HALLMARKS
1830-1900

R·Gray
S.COLLINS UTICA
S LEONARD
RICHARDS
SCOVIL & KINSEY
S.L.PRESTON
R.KEYWORTH
S&C
S.MARBLE
R·M
S.D.BROWER
Smith & Grant
R.MERRIMAN
Pure Coin
S.D.ROCKWELL
NEW YO
ROBT GRAY
SEYMOUR & HOLLISTER
S.P.SQUIRE
R·RAIT
S.F.YOUNG
LACONIA.NH
SA SA
S·H SH
SQUIRE & BROTHER OF CO
SAML KIRK
SK
SHAW & DUNLEVEY PHILA
Saml Kirk
S·HOYT
SHOYT.PEARL.ST
SB
BARRY
S.HOYT & CO
SQUIRE & LANDER
S.HUNTINGTON
S.BAKER
SK SK
S.REED S.REED
S·BOWNE S:BOWNE
S.KIRK S.KIRK S.Kirk

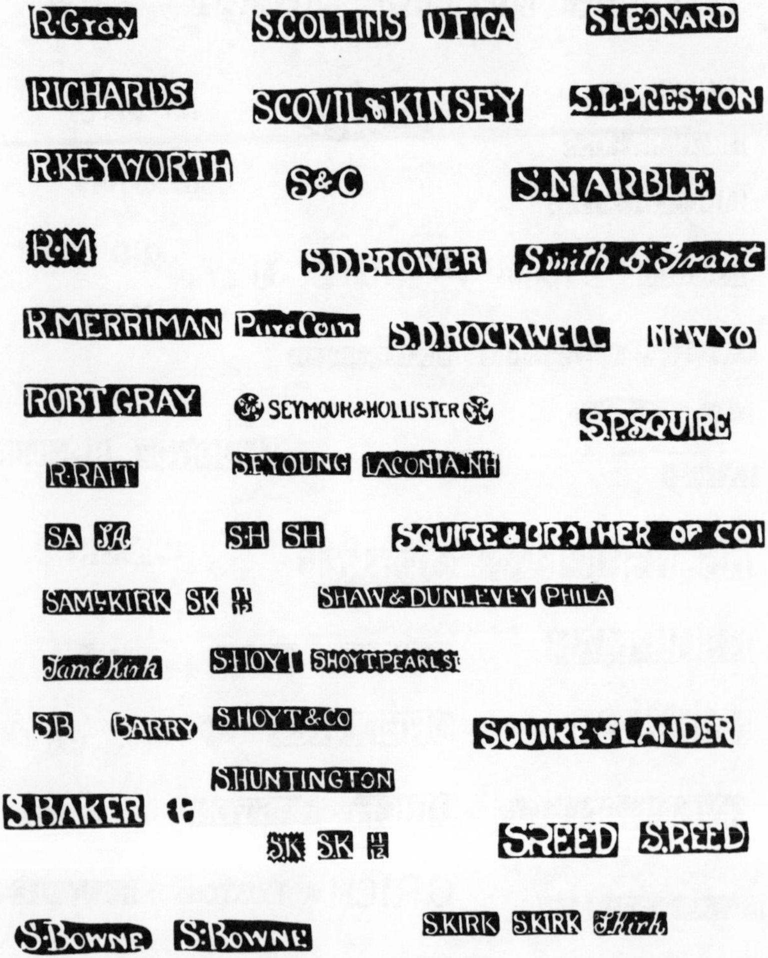

AMERICAN SILVERSMITHS HALLMARKS
1830-1900

Standish Barry   VERNON   W.F   [mark]   NEW YORK

STANTON   V.Marc VILLARD

STEPHENSON   V.LAFORME   W&C

STOCKMAN & PEPPER   V&W   W.FORBES NY   NY

S.WILMOT   W.ADAMS NEW-YORK

TA JA ARNOLD   WARD HARTFORT   W&G.SHARP

T.ARNOLD JA TA   W.A.RASCH NEW ORLEANS

    WATSON & BROWN   W&H

TAYLOR & LAWRIE   [mark]   W.A.WILLIAMS

TENNEY 251 BWAY

TERRY TERRY   W.B.N   WILMOT

Th.Farnam   W.C WC   [mark] WJ [mark]

T.K.MARSH PARIS.KY   W.C.DUSENBERR

T.W STERLING [mark]   WELLES & GELSTON

T.WARNER STERLING [mark]   WENTWORTH & CO

AMERICAN SILVERSMITHS HALLMARKS
1830-1900

WKENDRICK. LOUISVILL Wm.B Durgin CONCORD.N.I

W⁰ROGERS HARTFORD WM.ROGERS&SON WWG

W·S·N W.M⁰P.

W.S.P. W.S.PELLETREAU WW W.Ward

W⁰W·WHITE W.N.ROOT & BROTHER WOLFE & WRIGGINS

WOOD&HUGHES W.PITKIN

ZAHM & JACKSON WYER&FARLEY

STANDARD AND ASSAY MARKS—AMERICAN SILVER

Generally speaking the following marks were used from the end of the eighteenth century to the middle of the nineteenth. Two exceptions are Cesar Ghisel with his star in 1713 and Philip Syng with his leaf marks. The reason for many of these stamps is not obvious. *Authorities on the history of Baltimore Assay Marks advise that from 1814 to 1830, and later, all assaying and stamping was carefully supervised by specially elected silversmiths.

*Maryland Silversmiths. Dr. J. Hall Pleasants and Howard Sill. Old Plate. J.H. Buck.

Standard and Assay Marks 1810-1850

COURTESY: AMERICAN SILVERSMITHS, CRACKER BARREL PRESS

SILVER TERMINOLOGY & GLOSSARY

On the following pages you will find a complete listing and explanation of all terms and words used in Silver & Silverplate throughout this book.

These terms and words are also used in other books about Silver & Silverplate, and at auctions, antique shops, and museums and institutions having collections.

Acanthus: A form of ornamentation taken from the acanthus leaf, originally used on the Corinthian capital in the 1500's and 1600's.

Ajouré: A French term pertaining to metalwork which is perforated, pierced, or openwork.

Albata: Alloy of nickel, copper,a nd zinc, producing a silvery white metal; German silver, nickel silver.

Alcomy: An alloy of several base metals, primarily used in button making.

Alloy: A substance made up of two or more metals closely united, usually inter-mixed when molten.

Alpacca: An alloy of Copper, nickel, and zinc, also known as German silver and nickel silver.

Aluminum Silver: A composition of aluminum and silver which is much harder than aluminum, usually one of 3 parts silver and 97 parts aluminum.

Amorini: In Italian art, cupids or cherubs.

Amphora: Greek vase with ovoid-shaped body, broad shoulders, short neck, and loop handles.

Annealing: Reheating of silver to keep it malleable while it is being molded.

Anthemion: Greek honeysuckle.

Apocryphal: Classical term for a fraud, or a fake.

Applied: Pertaining to certain parts such as spouts, handles and covers which are sometimes made separately and applied with a solder.

Arabesque: A complex interwoven design of the Italian Renaissance.

Argentine: An alloy of tin and antimony used as a base for plating.

Argyle: A container for serving sauces, made with an inner jacket to hold hot water for the purpose of preserving heat; originally manufactured in silver.

Assay: A chemical test made to determine whether a metal is of the required quality.

Base metal: An alloy or metal of relatively low value to which a coating or plating is usually applied.

Beading: A border ornament made up of small, beadlike half-spheres; popular in the late 1700's.

SILVER TERMINOLOGY & GLOSSARY

Bell Metal: A type of Sheffield Plate consisting of a very heavy coating of silver, introduced in 1789 by Samuel Roberts.

Bleeding: Technical term pertaining to pieces of plate where the copper base is exposed.

Bobéche: Flat or saucer-shaped dish placed around candle base to catch wax drippings.

Bright-cut: A form of engraving popular in the late 18th century where metal is removed by cutting tools to give a faceted sparkle to the surface.

Bright Finish: Highly polished finish obtained by using jeweler's rouge on a polishing wheel.

Britannia: A silver-white alloy composed mainly of tin, copper, and antimony; sometimes contains a small quantity of zinc and bismuth; has a silvery appearance.

Bronze: An alloy composed mainly of copper and tin.

Buffing: Removing the outer layer of metal with a mechanical wheel to smoothe the surface of the metal.

Burnishing: Rubbing the surface with a tool to smoothe and harden the metal, increasing its durability.

Burnisher: Tool with hard, smooth working surface, used for burnishing gold and silver.

Butler's Finish: Finish obtained by wire wheel which makes tiny scratches, giving the surface a dull appearance.

Cable: Molding similar to twisted rope, derived from Norman architecture.

Cafe au lait Pots: Term referring to side-handled coffee dispensers from which hot milk and coffee are poured at the same time.

Chamberstick: A candle container used mainly as a lighting device in a bedroom.

Cann: A one-handled drinking container with no lid.

Cartouche: A motif in the shape of a shield or scroll with curled edges.

Caryatid: Statue of a woman used as a column.

Case: Formed in a mold.

Caudle Cup: A large two-handled bowl used in serving a wine-flavored gruel known as "caudle."

SILVER TERMINOLOGY & GLOSSARY

Chafing Dish: One dish inside another, the outer one filled with hot water and in direct contact with heat source, the inner one containing food.

Champleve: Enameling by cutting troughs in the metal into which the frit, or ground enamel, is melted; the surface is then ground and polished.

Chasing: A type of decorating produced by the use of chisels and hammers.

Ciborium: A goblet-shaped container used to hold the Eucharistic wafers.

Chasing: A type of decorating produced by the use of chisels and hammers.

Ciborium: A goblet-shaped container used to hold the Eucharistic wafers.

Cloisonne: Process of enameling by which the frit is melted into areas defined by wire soldered to the surface which is to be decorated.

Coin: Term used to indicate 900/1000 parts of silver and 100 parts of copper; this is the standard used for United States coins.

Commercial Silver: 999/1000 fine or higher.

Craig Silver: Used in making knives, similar to German silver.

C-scroll: Also known as "single scroll"; ordinarily applied to the shape of a handle in the form of a letter"c."

Cutler: One who deals in (makes, repairs, or sells) eating utensils or knives.

Cutlery: Knives with a cutting edge.

Date Letter: The insigne given by the London Goldsmiths Company to signify the particular year in which a piece of silver is manufactured.

Dish Cross: A silver or plate article used to support a porcelain bowl or dish ring, sometimes with an alcohol lamp for warming food.

Dish Ring: A round, pierced holder for a wooden or porcelain bowl, also known as a potato ring; originally of Irish descent.

Dolphin: Sculptured or carved motif using the sea dolphin.

Domed: Spheroid type of cover, first used in the early 18th century on tankards, teapots, and coffeepots.

Domestic Plate: Silverware used in the home, as opposed to that used in church services.

Double: French term used in designating silver plated ware.

Double-scroll: A line of reversed curves, used mainly in the design of handles.

SILVER TERMINOLOGY & GLOSSARY

Drawing Irons: Metal parts on a drawing bench through which silver is drawn.

Electrolysis: The process of conducting an electric current by an electrolyte of charged particles.

Electroplate: Term referring to articles made up of a base metal coated with silver produced by the process of electrolysis.

Electrotype: Reproduction of an art object made by electroplating a wax impression. Used greatly in the mid 1800's to reproduce antique articles.

Electrum: A natural pale yellow alloy of gold and silver; also an imitation alloy of silver made up of 8 parts copper, 4 parts nickel, and 3 1/2 parts zinc.

Embossing: Using only mechanical means to make raised impressions on the surface of a metal from the reverse side.

Engraving: Ornamentation produced by cutting lines in the silver.

EPBM: Electroplate on copper.

EPC: Electroplate on britannia metal.

Epergne: A centerpiece for the dining table usually consisting of a center dish surrounded by smaller dishes; French extraction.

EPNS: Electroplate on nickel silver.

EPNS-WMM: Electroplate on nickel silver with white metal mounts.

EPWM: Electroplate on white metal.

Etching: Surface ornamentation which is bitten-in with nitric acid.

Ewer: Pitcher or jug with a wide spout and a handle.

Feather Edge: A chased edge of slanting lines, usually used to ornament spoon handles.

Fine Pewter: A composition having a smooth surface, attractive color and strength, used for plate making; composed of 80 percent tin and 20 percent brass or copper.

Fine Silver: More than 999/1000 pure; too soft for most purposes, usually used as anodes or sheets for plating.

Finial: A crowning ornament on covers, often in figural form, animals, flowers, etc.

Flagoon: Large container used for serving wine or other liquors.

SILVER TERMINOLOGY & GLOSSARY

Flame: Term referring to a removable decoration used in place of a candle, usually in the center of a candelabra.

Flash Plate: Unbuffed, inexpensive plated ware.

Flat Chasing: Surface ornamentation in low relief; popular in England in early 1700's and very much used in America in the late 18th century.

Flatware: Generally refers to cutlery, such as knives, forks, spoons, and serving pieces, but may also be applied to plates, platters, and other flat articles.

Fluting: A form of grooving.

Fly Spoon: Spoon with a cut-out design in the bowl, used for removing flies or dirt from wine in chalice.

Folding Biscuit Box: A container having a center handle and two opening sides with screens; originally used during the Victorian period to keep and to serve muffins.

Forging: The molding of metal by heating and hammering.

Forged Marks: Term referring to fraudulent hallmarks stamped on a piece of silver.

French-grey finish: Finish obtained by giving article a light oxidation which is relieved with a steel crimped-wire wheel.

Fusion: Process of melting, as the fusion of metals, usually accomplished by applying intense heat.

Gadroon: A border ornamentation produced by notching or carving a rounded surface; also known as Knurling.

Galvanic Battery: A type of battery using direct currents of electricity named after Luigi Galvani.

Geometric: Angled line design.

German Silver: A silver-white alloy composed mainly of copper, zinc, and nickel; also referred to as nickel silver.

Gold Plating: Covering an article with gold.

Goldsmiths Company: The organization that regulates and conducts the silver industry.

Graver: Tool used for engraving silver.

Guilloche: A decorative motif of interlaced circular forms, usually having a flower in the center.

SILVER TERMINOLOGY
& GLOSSARY

Hallmark: The official mark used on articles of gold and silver by the English Goldsmiths Company to indicate their genuineness.

Hollow Handle: Handles made of two halves soldered together.

Hollow Ware: A general term applying to articles in the form of hollow vessels, such as bowls, pitchers, pots and mugs.

Husks: Festoons of seeds, such as in the Adam Style decoration.

Imperial Measure: Term used in England to indicate the legal standard weights and measures.

Ingot: Bar of silver or other metal.

Kilo: In the metric system, a prefix meaning thousand.

King's Head: A mark on a piece of silver denoting payment of a tax assessed by the crown.

Lasher Silver: Process whereby the copper and zinc is removed from the surface of nickel alloy, exposing only the nickel; invented by Thomas B. Lasher of the Holmes & Edwards Silver Company.

Latten: An alloy of copper and zinc; brass.

Limoges: Metal surface covered by enamel.

Maker's Mark: The insignia struck on a piece of silver or plate denoting the goldsmith or silversmith who produced it.

Malleable: Pliable, capable of being extended or molded by beating with a hammer.

Marrow Scoop: A long, thin silver utensil with a scoop center, used for extracting marrow from a bone.

Matte Finish: A dull surface produced by light hammering.

Metalsmith: One who knows the details of working with metal.

Monteith: A large bowl with serrated edges for chilling drinking glasses.

Motif: A prominent feature in the make-up of the work.

Mount: A decorative border.

Nickel Silver: An alloy of nickel, copper, and zinc: usually 65 percent copper, 5-25 percent nickel, and 10-30 percent zinc.

SILVER TERMINOLOGY
& GLOSSARY

Niello: Deep-line engraving on gold or silver, filled in with a type of black enamel.

Non-tarnishing Silver: Used mostly for jewelry, produced either by alloying silver with cadmium or by applying a thin plating of rhodium or palladium to the surface.

Nozzle: A socket for a candlestick.

N.S.: Nickel Silver.

Ormolu: Ground gold mixed with brass or bronze simulating gold in appearance.

Oxidizing: Application of an oxide to the metal to give shadows and depth.

Paten: Dish made of a precious metal for use in the Eucharistic service.

Patina: Soft luster appearance on surface of metal, usually due to age.

Peg Tankard: A vessel with measuring notches inside, used to hold ale or beer.

Piercing: Openwork decoration.

Pipkin: A container, usually with a handle extending at right angles, used for sauces.

Pix Box: A small vessel used to carry the host in Church Service.

Planishing: To use a planishing hammer to smoothe and cover hammer marks.

Plaque: A French term denoting thickness of plating.

Plate: Applies to articles made of precious metals; used mostly in England and on the Continent.

Plateau: A long, flat centerpiece equipped with a mirror.

Plating Vat: Tank used for the electrolysis of silver plated ware.

Plique-a-jour: Metal frames enclosing a translucent enamel with no metal backing.

Pricking: Delicate needlepoint engraving.

Pseudo Hallmarks: Devices used to simulate English hallmarks.

Raising: Creation of a piece of hollow ware starting with a flat circle of silver.

Repousse: Relief decoration hammered from inside of metal.

Revolving Tureen: Vessel with a roll cover and hot water compartment, originally used during the victorian Era.

SILVER TERMINOLOGY & GLOSSARY

Rococo: An extremely ornate style of decoration originated in France during the Louis XV period.

Rope-molding: A type of border, slightly spiraled, resembling a rope.

Royal Patronage: Encouragement of the Royal Family pertaining to trade.

R.P.: Rolled plate.

Satin Finish: Dull appearance obtained by using a revolving wheel of small wires.

Scorper: Small chisel with blades of different shapes, used for engraving.

Scroll: A spiralled ornamentation.

Serrated: Notched.

Sheffield Plate: Refers to plated articles produced by fusion.

Silver Edge: A solid silver border.

Silver Shield: The inserting of solid silver on plate to hold the engraving.

Silverite: According to advertisements, "A combination of tin, nickel, platinum, etc."

Silverplate: A base metal coated by electroplating with a layer of pure silver.

Snuffer: A flame extinguisher.

Solid Silver: 925/1000 silver and 75/1000 alloy (copper).

Soy Stand: A cruet or spice holder.

Spinning: Pressing a flat sheet of silver over a revolving lathe to produce hollow ware.

Stake: An iron anvil used to form silver objects.

Stamping Trademarks and Stock Numbers: System of stamping an article with a cipher preceeding the number, to ascertain whether the piece was nickel silver, silver soldered, or nickel silver with white metal mounts.

Stamping: Using heavy hammers to transfer designs from dies to the metal.

Sterling Silver: 925/1000 fine, with 75/1000 of added metal (usually copper) to give it strength and hardness.

SILVER TERMINOLOGY
& GLOSSARY

Stoning: Using an emery stone to shine silver.

Strapwork: Thin, folded, intertwined bands or straps.

Swaged: Molded by a process of rolling or hammering.

Syphon Stand: Pierced holder for seltzer water bottle.

Tempering: Using heat to strengthen metal.

Tinning: Working with tin, such as tin plating.

Touch: Silversmith's mark, made with a punch.

Touchstone: A hard stone or square of Wedgwood on which a piece of metal of known quality can be rubbed to compare its mark with that of a piece being estimated.

Town Mark: A city's insigne used as a hallmark to denote where the article was manufactured.

Trademark: Symbol or tradename identifying a manufacturer.

Trowel: Spade-shaped instrument, often made of silver and engraved.

Victorian Plate: Silver plated ware made by the process of electrolysis during the late 19th century.

Waiter: A serving or carrying tray.

White Metal: An alloy normally made up of two or more parts of the following elements: tin, copper, lead, antimony, and bismuth; the color gets whiter as more tin is added.

Winchester Measure: A system of measures by which early silver and silver plate drinking vessels were made; originated in Winchester, medieval capital of England.

Wine Cistern: A large vat used for holding vintage drinks.

Wine Funnel: A silver container with strainer and spout for pouring wine.

Wine Taster: A small vessel used by tasters at wineries to judge flavor and quality.

INTRODUCTION
ENGLISH SILVERSMITHS MARK

Although the bulk of this book is devoted to the products of American Silversmiths and Silver & Silverplate manufacturers, an understanding of English Silversmiths' marks, or hallmarks, is important to anyone interested in the subject of Silver.

There are four marks usually stamped or impressed on English silver in the following sequence: The Town, or Hall Mark indicating the location of the assay office; the Date Letter, or Annual Mark indicating when the piece was made; the Makers Mark, the initials of the silversmith in a shaped punch; the Standard, or Sterling Mark indicating Sterling quality.

Other marks found on English Silver are: Brittania Mark (1697 - 1719), required to indicate the higher standard of silver made during that time.

The Duty Mark, or Sovereign's Head (1784-1890) indicating that the duty had been paid on the item marked.

The Jubilee Mark added to pieces dated 1933/4 to 1935/6 to honor the silver Jubilee of King George V. and Queen Mary, and the Coronation mark of 1953 to indicate the acession of Queen Elizabeth II to the throne.

TOWN MARK	DATE LETTER	MAKERS MARK	STERLING MARK

ENGLISH STERLING SILVER AND SILVERPLATE

On the following pages is a representative cross-section of collectible English Sterling Silver and Silverplate. The pieces listed are dated from 1623 through 1925. Many of these items are still to be found in antiques shops, and at auctions, though they are rising in value and are increasingly scarce. Prices quoted are approximate current Retail Prices for items in Fine Condition.

ALL PICTURES ARE FROM THE VICTORIA & ALBERT MUSEUM, LONDON ENGLAND, AND ARE USED WITH PERMISSION.

ENGLISH STERLING SILVER & SILVERPLATE
Item, description, date   Retail

1. Bedroom candlestick, silver-gilt.
   Maker's mark: Paul de Lamerie. Hallmark: London.
   Circa 1748-9. 5 3/4" wide x 3 1/4" high..........................Set of 4 $3,000.00

2. Candlestick (1 of four), Sheffield plate,
   globe base, round baluster stem, shell ornament
   in relief. English, circa 1830 ....Pr. $300-400.00

3. Pair of candlesticks, silver, Birmingham hallmark 1906-7,
   maker's mark Liberty & Co. .... Pr $250-500.00

4. Candelabrum (1 of a pair), maker's mark "J.A.,"
   London hallmark 1819-20. 15 3/4" high................................ $2,040.00

5. Pair of silver candlesticks, hallmark, Dublin, circa 1704-6
   Tankard Sterling silver, hallmark, Dublin, circa 1710 .... $1,750.00

6. Candle snuffer and tray, silver. Maker's mark:
   "Thos. Robbins" on snuffer, "John Hawkes" on tray.
   Hallmark: London 1823-4. Tray 9 1/2" wide $240.00

7. Card carry case, electroplated silver panel gilt.
   Inscribed "Ellington Mason & Co. 1852.".............................. $25-50.00
   Ewer, electroplated silver, panel gilt, "Ellington's" $40-80.00

8. Cake basket, silver, Maker's mark "S. Herbert & Co."
   Hallmark "London 1753-4." $1500.00

9. Casket, sterling silver set with opals.
   Hallmark, Birmingham 1903. Maker's mark, "Liberty & Co."
   Designed by Archibold Knox. Art Nouveau............................ $1500.00

10. Sterling silver cup, hallmark, London 1623-4............................ $2000.00

11. Coffee pot, French sterling silver, Paris 1809-19 .... $750.00

12. Coffee pot, sterling silver, arms of "stacye,"
    wooden handle, English. Hallmark, London 1753-4 .... $1200.00

13. Sterling silver coffee pot, maker's mark:
    "David Smith & Robert Sharp," hallmark, London 1765-6.
    10 1/2" high x 9" wide $552.00

1.

2.

3.

5.

ENGLISH STERLING SILVER & SILVERPLATE

FOR
LISTINGS
PRICES
SEE
PAGE 60

4.

7.

7.

6.

8.

9.

10.

11.

12.

35.

35.

31.

32.

13.

14.

ENGLISH STERLING SILVER & SILVERPLATE
Item, description, date
Retail

14. Cruet stand, sterling silver with glass bottles,
maker's mark, "C.C.," hallmark,
London 1810-11. 5 7/8" wide $76.00

15. Christening cup, sterling silver, designed by
"R. Redgrave R.A.," hallmark, London 1865 ....$150-300.00

16. Cheese dish, mark of "Edward Wakelin,"
hallmark, London 1760. 14" wide. $500.00

17. Dish Ring, Sterling Silver, English,
circa 1730. 10 1/4" wide $350.00

18. Artichoke dish, sterling silver, hallmark,
London 1849-50. 3/4" high, 6 1/2" deep $200-400.00

19. Silver ewer, hallmark, London 1849-9, maker's mark,
"Joseph & Albert Savony." $450.00

20. Wine and Spirits labels, silver. English,
late 18th and 19th century ....Set $180.00

21. Silver wine labels. English, late 18th and 19th century ....Set $180.00

22. Wager cup, silver, maker's mark, "Jas. Walker,"
hallmark, Dublin 1706-8. 6 7/8" high $1250.00

23. Wine cooler, sterling silver,
maker's mark, "Frederick Kandler," hallmark, London 1775-6............$1500.00

23a Candlesticks, sterling silver, maker's mark,
"WC," hallmark, London 1771-2 ....Pair $850.00

24. Two-handled cup and cover, sterling silver, maker's mark,
"James Dixon & Son," hallmark, Sheffield 1859-60 ....$1500.00

25. Two "goats & bee" milk jugs, forged marks,
late 19th century, London hallmark. 4 1/2"high ....Pair $300.00

26. Inkstand sterling silver, hallmark, London 1845-6,
maker's mark, "Robert Hennell." $150.00-250.00

15.

16.

17.

18.

20.

19.

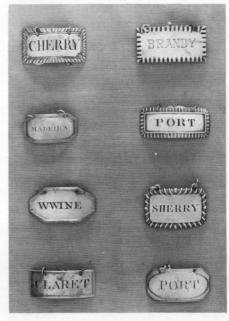

22.

21.

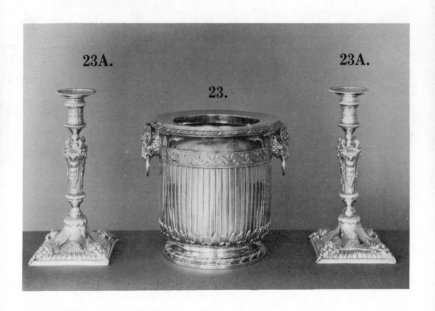

23A.

23A.

23.

24.

28.

27.

25.

ENGLISH STERLING SILVER & SILVERPLATE

Item, description, date	Retail

27. Jug, sterling silver, panel-gilt, hallmark, London 1881-2, maker's mark, "J. Aldwinkle & James Slater." $200.00

28. Kettle, stand and spirit burner, silver-plated copper. Designed by "Arthur Dixon for Birmingham Guild of Handicraft," circa 1905-10 .... $250.00

29. Mug, sterling silver panel-gilt, maker's mark, "Storr & Mortimer," hallmark, London 1810. 4" high $100-150.00

30. Mug, sterling silver, maker's mark, "Langlands & Robertson," hallmark, New Castle 1785 .... $150.00

31. Punch ladle, sterling silver bowl, whalebone handle. English, 18th century $43.00

32. Punch ladle, sterling silver, rosewood handle. Hallmark, London 1731-2 .... $84.00

33. Stirrup cup, sterling silver, mark of "W. Barwash & R. Sibley," hallmark, London 1827. 5 3/4" high $2500.00

34. Sterling silver salver, maker's mark, "Ja" (John Angell?), hallmark, London 1823-4 .... $1200-1500.00

35. Pair of sterling silver sauce bowls, maker's mark, "B.E." (?), hallmark, London 1751-2. Arms engraved $600-450.00

36. *Salt cellar, sterling silver, hallmark, London 1695-6. 2 1/2" high.. Pr. $500.00

37. *Salt cellar, sterling silver, English, second half of the 17th century. 1 1/8" high .... Pr. $500.00

38. *Salt cellar, sterling silver, made by "Simon Pantin," hallmark, London 1707-8. 2 5/8" wide .... Pr. $300-600.00

39. Sterling silver sconce, hallmark, London 1703-4, engraved maker's mark, "John Rand.".............................. Pr. $3500.00

36.

38.   37.

ENGLISH STERLING SILVER & SILVERPLATE

29.

30.

33.

34.

40.

41.

39.

Item, description, date	Retail

40. Teapot, sterling silver, hallmark, London 1830,
maker's mark, "TW,WM." $150-350.00

41. Teapot, silver, hallmark, Birmingham 1861-2,
maker's mark, "John Hardman & Co." $150-250.00

42. Teapot, sterling silver, maker's mark,
"A. Fogelberg," hallmark, London 1778-9. 5" high...................... $400.00

43. Tea caddy, sterling silver, hallmark, London 1831-2 .... $500-700.00

44. Tea service, sterling silver, wooden knobs
and handles. Designed and made by "Christian Dell"
(b 1893) at metal workshop of Bauhaus 1925 .... $850.00

45. Tankard, sterling silver, maker's mark,
"Anthony Nelme," hall mark, London 1698.
7" high, diameter of base, 4 5/8"...................................... $1920.00

46. Silver tankard, maker's mark, "W. Shaw & W. Priest,"
hallmark, London 1756-7. 6 1/4" high.................................. $564.00

47. Tea and coffee service, sterling silver,
hallmark, London 1868,
maker's mark, "Robert Hennell." $1032.00

48. Tea and coffee service, sterling silver,
hallmark, London 1872,
maker's mark, "W.G. Sissons." $1000-1500.00

49. Tankard, electroplate silver designed
by "Alfred Stevens," circa 1870 for the old Restaurant
Victoria & Albert Museum $25-50.00

ENGLISH STERLING SILVER & SILVERPLATE

43.

45.

42.

44.

ENGLISH STERLING SILVER & SILVERPLATE

47.

49.

46.

48.

AMERICAN SILVER & SILVERPLATE HOUSEHOLD ITEMS

TABLE OF CONTENTS

AMERICAN SILVER & SILVERPLATE

BELLS

Among the most popular of small collectables are bells of all types. Table and call bells were made of glass and china, but the most collected bells are of metal: brass, copper, silver and silverplate.

Table and tea bells of silver and silverplate were made by most American manufacturers in a great variety of designs and shapes, from simple half-round with plain cast handle, to the most elaborate engraved, embossed, and chased examples with figural handles.

CALL BELLS

Call bells on a base, or legs, have a spring activated clapper that was activated by pressing the button to call a maid or servant. Most are made of silverplate.

TEA BELLS

Sterling Silver—$20.00—$50.00
Silverplate—$7.50—$20.00

CALL BELLS

Plain—$5.00—$15.00
Ornate—$7.50—25.00

Nº 036

Nº 037

Nº 040

Nº 039

Nº 041

Nº 038

Nº 042
"old Florentine"

Nº 048

Nº 046

Nº 047

Nº 044

Nº 045

STERLING SILVER AND CUT CRYSTAL

Listed and priced below, and illustrated in the full page photo are a representative cross-section of the Sterling Silver and cut crystal pieces encountered in antique shops, auctions, and galleries.

These items were produced during the period 1870—1920, by all the American Silver manufacturers. The glass and crystal containers were made in both Europe and the United States, and were combined into these articles by the silver manufacturer.

Item, description date	Retail
1. Cut crystal boudoir jar with sterling silver repousse top, Art Nouveau motif, floral	$25-45.00
2. Same as above	
3. Toothbrush holder with crystal and sterling silver Art Nouveau floral motif	$21.00
4. Unusually-shaped cut crystal vase with sterling silver rim; Victorian motif, circa 1880's	$60.00
5. Cut crystal boudoir jar, sterling silver engraved top	$25-45.00
6. Art Nouveau dresser mirror, silver plated, typical dragonfly,lilypond and frog motif	$210.00
7. Cut crystal boudoir jar with sterling silver, initial-engraved top	$25-45.00
8. Crystal boudoir jar with sterling silver top	$25-45.00
9, 18, 21, 22, 23, 24, 25 & 26. Eight piece etched crystal and sterling silver travel set: Cologne bottle, pin box, hand mirror, soap dish, brush, powder bottle, button hook, nail file; circa 1900	Set $250.00
10. Crystal and sterling silver travel hairpin box	$15.00
11. Cut crystal boudoir jar, sterling silver floral motif top	$25-45.00
12. Same as above.	
13. Crystal with silver overlay, Heisey glass, sterling silver top	$25-45.00
14. Cut crystal perfume bottle, sterling silver repousse top	$45.00
15. Same as above.	
16. Small cut crystal boudoir jar. Sterling silver, initial engraved on top	$20-35.00
17. Crystal perfume bottle, heavy sterling silver overlay	$25-45.00
19. Cut crystal and pierced sterling silver tray, Victorian	$65.00
20. Small cut crystal boudoir jar, sterling silver Art Nouveau top	$20-35.00

STERLING SILVER AND CUT CRYSTAL

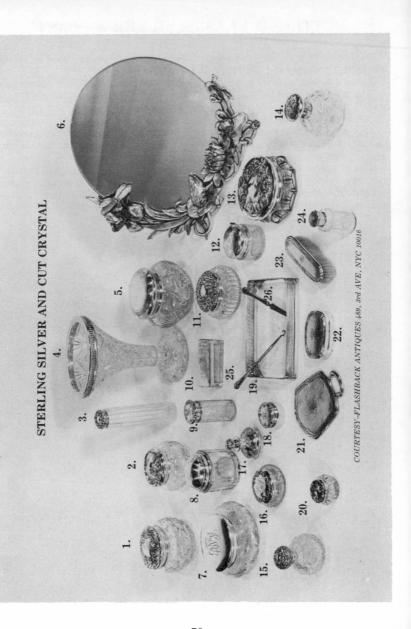

COURTESY—FLASHBACK ANTIQUES 489, 3rd AVE, NYC 10016

79

BOTTLES & FLASKS, SILVER & GLASS

The combination of Silver, Silverplate and glass of all types reached its zenith during the Victorian and Art Nouveau periods.

Flasks and bottles of all types in cut, pressed, or engraved glass were made in a large variety of designs and patterns, with Sterling or Silverplate tops and often with the bottle seated in a Sterling or Silverplate base, or completely encased in an open fretwork of floral or Rococo design.

This same production technique was used on many colognes and perfume bottles and toilet and atomizer bottles. A blank plaque for engraving initials was usually centered on the fretwork.

Vinaigrettes, or salt bottles, Glass Puff Boxes, Inkwells, Mucilage bottles and toothbrushes are a part of this highly desirable, valuable and collectable group.

Cut and engraved glass claret jugs with ornate silver handle and pourer, and green-glass brandy decanters encased in floral and Rococo design open fretwork silver were popular in the mid 1850's and are sought by both bottle and silver collectors.

GLOVE COLOGNES

A charming and highly collectable type of Victorian and Art Nouveau bottle are the Glove Colognes. Their slender, tapered shapes enabled them to be worn in the Victorian ladies glove. These miniature cologne receptacles were objects of much decorative art usually with flower motifs, engraved, chased, and embossed on the surface.

BOTTLES & FLASKS—SILVER & GLASS

Silver & Cut Crystal Colognes & Perfume Bottles
*Retail $25.00—$75.00

*Price Depends On Size Of Bottle

BOTTLES & FLASKS—SILVER & GLASS

Silver & Cut Crystal Liquor Flasks
*Retail $45.00—$85.00

*Silver Overlay & Crystal Cologne Bottles $25.00—$65.00

*Price Depends On Size of Bottles

BOTTLES & FLASKS—SILVER & GLASS

Silver Overlay & Crystal Flasks
*Retail $25.00—$50.00

**Silver & Cut Crystal
Perfume Bottles**
*Retail
$20.00—$40.00

*Price Depends On Size of Bottles

BOXES—SILVER & SILVERPLATE

The bewildering array of boxes for every purpose and in every style and design attests to the Victorian love of these practical table appointments. Every Silver and Silverplate manufacturer made them as music boxes and for Jewelry, gloves, cards, candy, cigars, tobacco, handkerchiefs, stamps, nick-nacks, trinkets, sewing items, pins, powder and cosmetics, etc.

They were made in all shapes and sizes with square or rectangular predominating. Designs ran the gamit from Classic to Rococo, in embossing, engraving, etc., and during the Art Nouveau period the *box itself* was made with curvy undulating surfaces and typical floral and female nude motifs. Many of the Victorian boxes had cast novelty figural motifs and ingenious hinged drawers and swinging covers that could be opened by pushing a Cupid on a swing, a bird on a perch, etc. Cut glass inserts; Amberina, Ruby, Malachite, etc., in boxes and Silverplate mounts are most desirable and valuable, and the most difficult to find.

Silverplate Boxes In Fine Working Condition
*Retail—$30.00—$75.00
*Depending On Size Of Box
And Decoration

Boxes in Fine Working Condition   *Retail $30.00—$75.00

BOXES—SILVER & SILVERPLATE

*Retail
Silverplate
$15.00-$40.00

Sterling Silver
$25.00-$125.00

*Depending on Size
& Decoration

BOXES
SILVER & SILVERPLATE

**ART
NOUVEAU
CIRCA
1909**

**Martele
Silver**

ART NOUVEAU
STERLING SILVER
$65.00

*Depending On Size & Decoration

BOXES—SILVER & SILVERPLATE
TOBACCO & SNUFF BOXES

*Retail
Sterling Silver—$20.00-$40.00
Silverplate—$15.00-$30.00

NOVELTY BOXES

*Retail
Silverplate—$15.00-$40.00

*Depending On Size,
Decoration & Condition

BOXES—SILVER & SILVERPLATE

*Retail
Silverplate
$40.00-$60.00
In Fine
Working
Condition

*Retail
Silverplate—$15.00-$30.00

*Price Depends on Size, Design & Condition

BRIDES' BASKETS

"Brides' Baskets" is a name applied to berry or fruit dishes made with an insert bowl of glass. Originally the Brides' Baskets were made of silver and silver gilt with pierced openwork, overall designs of flowers and with a carrying handle in the form of a silver ribbon bowknot. Fresh flowers could be placed in the basket. These Sterling silver fancies were made by Tiffany, Gorham, etc.

The Silverplate pieces were made by Meriden Brittania, Rogers & Bros., Wilcox Silver Co., and others with a frame standing on flour low feet, a "basket handle" attached. Handles and stands were richly decorated in Rococo, Victoriand, and Classic motifs. The glass inserts were made in many patterns, from pressed, etched, and cut clear or frosted glass. Much imported colored and Art Glass were used, including Amethyst, Agata, Amberina, Burmese, Cranberry, Peachblow, Pomona, Rubina Verde, Mary Gregory, etc. In the mid 1880's the ruffled, fluted irregular edge become popular. Complete original "Brides Baskets" of this period are difficult to find. The desirability of the Art glass inserts resulted in collectors separating them from the Silverplated mounts. Imported reproductions are made and sold, reputable dealers would be the best source for orginal "Brides' Baskets."

BRIDES' BASKETS—SILVERPLATES & GLASS

*Retail
With Clear Glass
$45.00—$65.00
With Cranberry Glass
$100.00—$200.00
With Pink Glass
$150.00—$200.00
With Satin Glass
$175.00—$300.00

*For Original
Frames &
Glass In
Fine Condition

CIRCA
1880

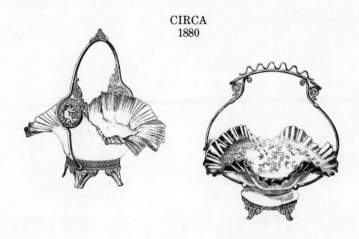

See Page 91 for Retail Prices

BRIDES' BASKETS—SILVERPLATE & GLASS

See Page 91 For Retail Prices

CANDELABRA—SILVER & SILVERPLATE

As a natural outgrowth of the single candlestick, the candelabra with its graceful arms was the decorative table lighting source of the 1700's and 1800's. In the latter half of the 1700's elaborate massive candelabras were made for the great houses of England and the Continent. Magnificent pieces with up to twelve lights were made for dining halls of wealth and aristocracy.

Sheffield plate, silver, and silverplate candelabras varied greatly in design and decoration reflecting the times, though the majority consisted of two branches with the center support having a removable finial and socket into which a third candle fitted. Candelabra with twisted and removable branches were a feature of Victorian dining tables enabling the multiple use of the individual elements; as seven, five, and three light units or individual candlesticks. Candelabra of typical Art Nouveau design used nudes, flowing hair ladies, floral forms, etc.

*Retail
Silverplate
2 Arm—$15.00-$30.00 Each
3 Arm—$20.00-$40.00 Each
4 Arm—$50.00-$100.00 Each
5 Arm—$75.00-$200.00 Each

*Retail
†Sterling Silver
2 Arm—$35.00-$70.00 Each
3 Arm—$50.00-$125.00 Each
4 Arm—$75.00-$200.00 Each
5 Arm—$200.00-$500.00 Each

†Depending on Silver Weight

*Prices Depend on Size, Design, Condition

CANDELABRA

Note: Prices
Quoted For Single
Pieces—Pairs
Are Worth
Double-Plus

ART
NOUVEAU
CIRCA 1904
Silverplate
$150.00

Art Nouveau candelabrum designed & patented by Albert Steffin, Assigned to the Pairpoint Corp. (Design Patent 36,875; April 12, 1904)

CANDELABRA

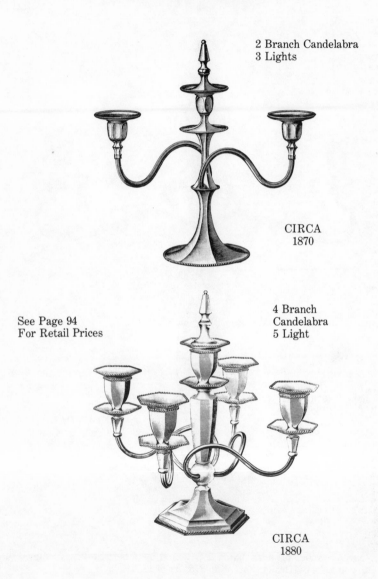

2 Branch Candelabra
3 Lights

CIRCA
1870

See Page 94
For Retail Prices

4 Branch
Candelabra
5 Light

CIRCA
1880

CANDELABRA

ART NOUVEAU
CIRCA 1904

Silverplate
5 Branch
Candelabra

See Page
94 for Prices

CANDELABRA

6 Branch
7 Lights

Art Nouveau—Martele Silver—CIRCA 1906
See Page 94 for Prices

SILVER & SILVERPLATE
CANDLESTICKS

The history of candle holders pre-dates Christian civilization.

As an important adjunct to Christian liturgy the candle holder reached a peak of artistic excellence during the period 500 A.D. to 1600, with elaborate designs in gold, silver, and precious stones. Many examples are on view in museums and churches. Cast simple candlesticks were made in large numbers in the early 1700's. These had gadrooned mouldings and were made of solid Sterling Silver. While styles in candlesticks were subject to the same influences as other Silver artifacts, the main thrust of design was Greek classic copied from the Ionic columns with fluted pillars and scrolled capitals.

Rococo motifs of the George II period introduced elaborate curlicues, swags, cartouches and floral embellishments. The classic and Rococo were the two primary design sources for Sheffield Plate and American candlesticks of the Victorian era. By the 1860's American Silverplate manufacturers were producing candlesticks in a large variety of sizes, shapes, and designs, including the typical Victorian use of cast figures such as mythological and literary characters, exotic birds and animals and fruits and flowers.

Handled candlesticks of this period were low socket candleholders on a drip disk, handles and bases were often heavily embellished.

The structure of Art Nouveau candlestick admirably combined the undulating female figure, long flowing hair, and floral and sea motifs. Again the Martele pieces individually created by the Gorham craftsmen are the most beautiful and valuable to be found. Candlesticks are sought and collected in pairs or sets of four.

CANDLESTICKS—SILVER & SILVERPLATE

CIRCA
1880

*Retail
Silverplate
$15.00-$40.00 Pair
Silver
$50.00-$200.00 Pair

*Chamber
Candlestick
Silverplate
$8.00-$15.00
Silver
$15.00-$40.00

Silver
$35.00-$60.00

*Depending on Height, Design, Weight of Silver.

CANDLESTICKS

ART
NOUVEAU
CANDLE
STICKS

Silver
12" high
Retail
$225.00 Pair
CIRCA 1900

MARTELÉ
GORHAM

CHAMBERSTICKS & SNUFFERS

As the name implies these portable handled candle holders were made to light the way to the bed chamber of homes of the 1700's and 1800's. Early Silver and Silverplate models had a scissors type of snuffer, later the familiar "Dunce-Cap" conical snuffer was extensively used, and are more available to the collector.

*Retail
Silverplate—$12.50-$30.00
Silver—$28.50—$75.00

MARTELÉ
GORHAM

ART NOUVEAU
CIRCA 1902
$85.00-$150.00
Sterling Silver

*Price Depends on Design, Condition & Weight of Silver

CHAMBERSTICKS & SNUFFERS

*Retail

Sterling Silver—$85.00-$150.00

ART NOUVEAU
MARTELE
CIRCA 1902

*Prices Depend on
Design, Condition,
& Silver Weight.

CARD TRAYS—CARD RECIEVERS

From the mid 1850's to World War I, card trays, or receivers, were made by every major silver plate manufacturer in an enormous variety of designs. The early ones were quite plain, but they evolved into etched, chased, embossed, hammered, and enameled trays, embellished with birds, animals, flowers, cherubs. Art glass vases set in holders were often combined with the trays.

*Retail
Silverplate—$25.00-$75.00
*Depending On Size & Decoration
Silverplate & Art Glass—$50.00-$200.00
*Depending on Glass, Size & Decoration

CARD RECEIVERS

Silverplate—CIRCA 1865-1880

Silverplate & Art Glass

CARD TRAYS & RECEIVERS

Silverplate
CIRCA 1865-1880
*Retail
$20.00—$75.00
Sterling Silver
Double Price

*Depending on Size
& Decoration, & Condition

CARD TRAYS

Silverplate
& Art Glass

Retail
$125.00

*Retail
Sterling Silver
$50.00-$150.00

Silverplate
CIRCA 1865-1880
*Retail
$25.00-$75.00

*Prices for fine condition

CARD CASES

Card cases were carried by fashionable ladies of the Victorian era. American silver and silver plate makers produced them in a large variety of designs with floral or bird motifs engraved or embossed. Chains were attached so the cases could be carried. Plush or Morrocco boxes, into which the cases fit, were often sold with the cases.

*Retail
Silverplate
$10.00-$30.00
Depending
On Decoration

Silver
$20.00-$65.00
Depending
On Decoration

Coin
Silver
Same Prices
As Silver

CARD CASES

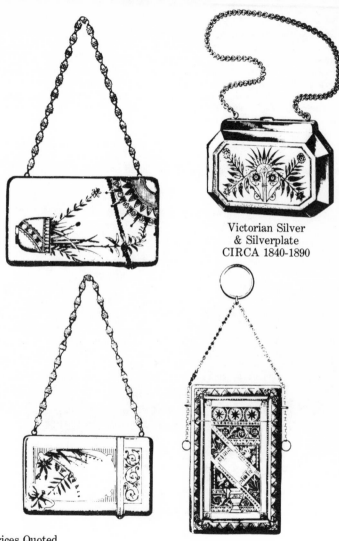

Victorian Silver
& Silverplate
CIRCA 1840-1890

*Prices Quoted
Are For Fine Condition

CENTERPIECES—MANTEL ORNAMENTS

A great variety of these cast figures were produced in the 1880's and 1890's. They ranged in size from a few inches to two feet in height. The subjects ranged over many areas representing mythological and classic figures: Apollo, Mars, Dying Gladiator, Arabs, Indian Chief, Indian Squaw, etc., animals of all types, domestic and wild; dogs, deer, wolves, buffalo, lions, bears, etc.

These cast figures were usually made of so-called "White Metal," and silver plated, or gold or gilt plated. Some were made of Sterling Silver, such as the Gorham Mfg. Co. Martele centerpiece with nymph figure handles and Art Nouveau floral decorations.

Though these ornaments were made for decorative purposes, many of these same figures appeared on mantel cocks of the period. They were also adapted to use as lamp bases and these pieces are found with holes drilled.

*Retail

Silverplate—$20.00-$100.00
*Depending on Size & Subject
American Indians Are Most Valuable

Silver—$100.00-$300.00
*Depending on Size & Silverweight

GORHAM
MARTELÉ
Retail—$300.00

ART
NOUVEAU
CIRCA 1895

CENTERPIECES

*Retail
Silverplate
$20.00-$100.00
Silver
$100.00-$300.00

*Prices
Quoted
For Fine
Condition

CENTERPIECES—MANTLEPIECES

*Prices Depend
On Size & Subject
& Weight of Silver

CENTERPIECES—MANTLEPIECES

Retail

Silverplate **$20.00-$100.00**
Silver **$100.00-$300.00**

American Indian Subjects
Are Most Valuable

ALL CENTERPIECES
CIRCA 1865-1880

CHILDREN'S SILVER & SILVERPLATE

Small porringers and "Pap Boats" and "Pap Spoons" were child feeding implements used in the 1700's. These were made by American silversmiths and often had engraved simple designs.

By the 1850's the popularity of silver children's items as gifts for children and their parents resulted in a proliferation of many products. These included: Bowls, porringers, pap boats, pap spoons, cup sets, christening sets, whistles, rattles, napkin rings, spoons, etc.

Nursery rhymes were the source of much of the design and embellishments used on these pieces. Etching, engraving, chasing, repousse, and embossing were the techniques used to decorate children's items. Animals of all types, especially dogs and cats, were also a popular motif.

During the 1930's Mickey Mouse, Donald Duck, and other cartoon characters were used as subjects on silver children's spoons, forks, and sets. These are sought after by collectors of Disney and Comic characters.

The Gorham Silver Company produced many children's items. The most expensive and unique were the Martele pieces; plates, mugs, porringers, etc., individually made by Gorham silversmiths.

Children's silverware items are a good area of endeavor for the new collector.

*Retail
Silverplate
Rattles & Whistle, etc.—**$10.00-$25.00**
Baby Brush, Combs, etc.—**$12.50-$30.00**
Cups, Spoons, Porringers—**$8.50-$20.00**

Sterling Silver
Rattles, Rattle & Whistle, etc.—**$15.00-$20.00****
Baby Brush, Combs, etc.—**$20.00-$60.00**
Cups, Spoons, Porringers—**$10.00-$50.00**

*Price Depends On Design, Size, Condition
**If Made with ivory, Mother of Pearl, etc.

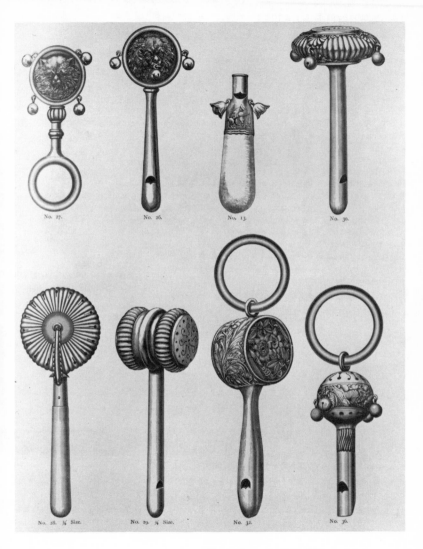

No. 27.

No. 26.

No. 13.

No. 30.

No. 28. ¼ Size.

No. 29. ¼ Size.

No. 32.

No. 36.

For prices see page 114.

CHILDREN'S SILVER ITEMS

BABY WHISTLE & RATTLE

BABY RATTLE

BABY BRUSH

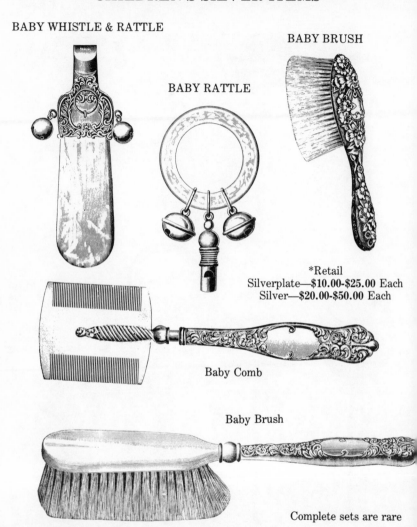

*Retail
Silverplate—$10.00-$25.00 Each
Silver—$20.00-$50.00 Each

Baby Comb

Baby Brush

Complete sets are rare

*Prices depend on Decoration & Condition

CHILDREN'S SILVER CUPS

Retail
ART NOUVEAU SILVER CUPS
CIRCA 1895
$25.00-$60.00 Each
Depending on Size & Decoration

CHILDREN'S SILVER & SILVERPLATED CUPS

*Retail
Silverplate $10.00-$25.00
Silver $25.00-$60.00

*Price Depends on
Condition & Decoration

CIRCA
1870-1890

118

CHILDRENS CUPS
SILVERPLATE
& SILVER

*Retail
Silverplate **$10.00-$25.00** Each
Silver **$25.00-$60.00** Each

Note: Cups With
Matching Spoons
Are Rare & Valuable

CIRCA
1870-1890

CHILDREN'S SILVER
COMIC CHARACTER 2 PIECE SETS

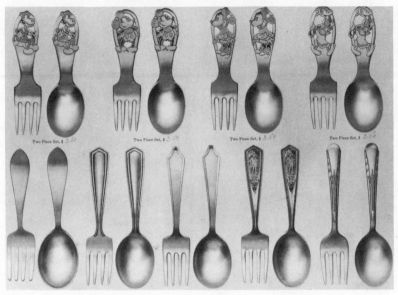

Two Piece Set, $ 3.50   Two Piece Set, $ 3.50   Two Piece Set, $ 3.50   Two Piece Set, $ 3.50

Comic Character Spoons & Forks Silver—**$3.50** Each

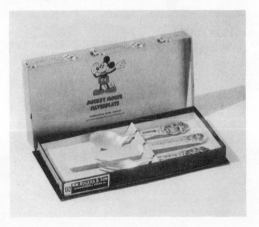

Mickey
Mouse
Childs'
Set
$30.00
Silverplate

FERN DISHES & FLOWER POTS

The Victorian love of flowers and green plants manifested itself in these silver-plated fern dishes and flower pots, that held linings of porcelain, pottery, and metal. Most fern dishes were round in shape but oblong shapes are known. They often had handles attached to the outside casings and sat on low feet. Designs were Victorian Rococo frequently in open fretwork. Flower pots were similar in form and design to Fern Dishes though they were taller and usually had a flat base.

*Retail
Silverplate—$30.00-$80.00
Depending on Size & Decorations

Silver—$60.00-$200.00
*Depending on Size, Weight of
Silver & Decorations

CIRCA
1870

Fern Dish

FERN DISHES & FLOWER POTS

Fern Dish

Flower Pot

Fern Dish

Fern Dish

CIRCA
1870 to
1900

FERN DISHES & FLOWER POTS

CIRCA
1870 to
1900

Flower Pot

*Retail
Silverplate
$30.00-$80.00
Silver
$60.00-$200.00
Depending
On Size &
Weight&
Design

Fern Dish

Fern Dish

STERLING SILVER AND SILVERPLATE TABLE ITEMS

See color picture on page 132

Item, description, date	Retail

1. BUD VASE, MINIATURE.
   6" high, sterling silver,
   "trumpet" shape. Circa 1900's $18-28.00

2. SALVER.
   Silver plate, 10" circumference with
   engraved dedication.
   Hallmark: "Reed & Barton"
   Circa 1899. .... $15-30.00

3. CAKE PLATES.
   Silver plate, grape and leaves motif
   on rim. Hallmark: "S. & Co."
   (Sheffield Silver Co., Brooklyn, N.Y.)
   Circa 1910 .... Set of a dozen $150-200.00
   Each $15-25.00

4. BUD VASES.
   Sterling silver, floral motif art
   nouveau base. Victorian cut glass, enameled and
   hand painted, 24 kt. gold trim......................... Pair $350-450.00

5. INDIVIDUAL CAKE PLATE $15-25.00

6. SOUP LADLE.
   Silver plate grape and leaf rim design.
   Hallmark: "Benedict" Circa 1890 .... $30.00

7. CAKE PLATE.
   Silver plate grape and leaf rim design.
   Hallmark: "Benedict" Circa 1898 .... $35-75.00

8. BLOWN CRYSTAL VASE.
   Pierced silver overlay, enamel rim.
   French hallmark. Circa 1890 .... $170-250.00

AMERICAN SILVER & SILVERPLATE
TABLE ITEMS

Item description, date   **Retail**

9. SUGAR TONGS.
Sterling silver, stamped and chased
Victorian floral motif. Circa 1870 .... $15-35.00

10. DEMI-TASSE SPOON.
Sterling Silver "Daffodil" pattern.
Hallmark: "Gorham." $10-20.00

11. BERRY SPOON.
Sterling silver, pierced and engraved,
floral motif, scalloped edge $12-15.00

12. PICKLE FORK.
Sterling silver, pierced and engraved......................... $12-15.00

13. LADIES SWORD HAT PIN.
Sterling silver. Circa 1890's $12-20.00

14. LADIES CALLING CARD CASE.
Sterling silver, drawn wire roccoco design.
Circa 1890's $25-50.00

15. LADIES EVENING PURSE MIRROR.
Sterling silver, flowing hair art nouveau motif.
Circa 1890's $30-75.00

16. SHOE HORN.
Sterling silver, art nouveau motif.
Circa 1880's $25-40.00

17. TEAPOT.
Sterling silver, copy of George II period pot.
Rosewood handle and finial.
Hallmark: "Gorham" Circa 1880's $125.00

18. SUGAR BOWL.
2 handled sterling silver,
copy of George II period bowl.
Hallmark: "Gorham." $45.00

STERLING SILVER AND SILVER-PLATE TABLE ITEMS

See color picture on page 135

Item, description, date	Retail
1. TWO HANDLED VASE OR LOVING CUP. Sterling silver, American-made reproduction of George I English original. Chased and engraved. Weight: 22 1/2 ounces. Hallmark: "Howard & Co." Circa 1897	$325.00
2. *"BRIDES BASKET." Silver plated base and handle. Pressed clear glass, scalloped edge. Hallmark: "Rogers Bros." Circa 1880's	$75-135.00
3. **PICKLE CASTOR WITH TONGS. Silver plated base, handle and tongs. Pressd clear glass bottle, "Finecut" pattern Hallmark: "Rogers Bros." Circa 1880's	$60-100.00
4. WATER PITCHER. Silver plated over Brittania metal, Victorian floral engraving. Hallmark: "Reed & Barton - No. 460" Circa 1870's	$85.00
5. FRUIT OR NUT BOWL. Sterling Silver, Victorian 3 and 4 leaf clover and chrysanthemum motif. Hallmark: "Tiffany & Co.-T" Circa 1890's	$60-100.00
6. HANDLED FRUIT BASKET. Silver plated, pierced basket and handle. Hand-made rope gallery (rim of basket). Hallmark: "Rogers Bros." Circa 1869	$85-125.00

* *Note: "BRIDES BASKET in other types of art glass (opaline, amethyst, webb) are more valuable.*

** *Note: PICKLE CASTORS with art glass inserts, amberina, cranberry burmese, rubina verde, are much more valuable.*

STERLING AND COIN SILVER
AND SILVER PLATE
See Color Picture on Page 136

Item, description, date	Retail

1, 2 & 3. 3 PIECE TEA OR COFFEE SET. Sugar bowl, waste bowl, creamer, footed with beaded rim. All silver plate, quadruple. Hallmark: "E.G. Webster & Son," circa 1880's ....Set $145.00

4. CREAMER. Silver plate, footed. Hallmark: "D.S." (Dirksen Silver Co.?) Circa 1890's $12-17.00

5. & 6. CREAMER & SUGAR BOWL. Sterling silver, hollow moulding handle, ball and scroll design. Hallmark: "Gorham."...Set of 2 $65.00

7. CHILD'S MUG. Sterling silver, Victorian period. Hallmark: "Gorham." $15-20.00

8. TABLE CENTERPIECE. Sterling silver, carved African jungle scene, palm trees, native, lion, on Ebony base. Victorian, circa 1860's $250.00

9. CARVING SET. Sterling silver, "Anniversary" pattern. Hallmark: "I.S." (International Silver—1847 Rogers Bros.) Circa 1920 ....Set of 2 $45-55.00

10. DINNER FORKS. Sterling silver, set of 6, "Aldine" pattern. Hallmark: "Rogers & Hamilton." Circa 1895 ....Set of 6 $40-60.00

11. DINNER KNIVES. STERLING SILVER, SET OF ¾, "Aldine" pattern Hallmark: "Rogers & Hamilton." Circa 1895 ....Set of 6 $60-100.00

12. DINNER TEA SPOONS. Sterling silver, set of 6, "Mayflower" pattern. Hallmark: "Rogers XII." Circa 1903 ....Set of 6 $45-65.00

13. PICKLE FORK. Sterling silver, pierced and engraved "Dunraven" pattern. Hallmark: "Rogers." Circa 1895 ....$12-15.00

14. BERRY SPOON. Sterling silver, pierced and engraved floral motif. "Yale" pattern. Circa 1886....................................$12-15.00

15. DEMI-TASSE SPOON. Sterling silver, "Daffodil" pattern. Hallmark: "Gorham." $12-15.00

16. SUGAR TONGS. Sterling silver, stamped and chased. Victorian floral motif. Circa 1870 ....$15-35.00

17. & 18. SUGAR SPOONS. Coin silver. Hallmark: "J.G. Victorian & Son." Circa 1810 ....Each $25.00

19. CAKE SERVER. Sterling silver, "Anniversary" pattern. Hallmark: I.S." (International Silver-1847 Rogers Bros.) Circa 1920 ....Set of 2 $45-55.00

STERLING AND COIN SILVER
AND SILVER PLATE
See Color Picture on Page 136

20. SOUP LADLE. Sterling silver, "Anniversary" pattern.
Hallmark: "I.S." Circa 1920 ....$15-20.00
21. SERVING FORK. Sterling silver, "Anniversary" pattern.
Hallmark: "I.S." Circa 1920 ....$15-30.00
22. SOUP SPOON. Coin silver. Hallmark: "P. Miller"
"Providence, R.I." Circa 1810...$50.00

Man's Pocket Watch
Circa 1905

Ladies
Art Nouveau
Mirror

Ladies
Art Nouveau
Flask

Ladies
Victorian
Mirror

Victorian & Art Nouveau
Silver

SILVER CARD CASE, MATCH SAFES, WATCH & CHAIN
Victorian & Art Nouveau Match Safes

For Listing & Pricing See Page 235

Victorian
Silver
Card
Carry
Case

Art Nouveau
Silver Watch
& Chain

SILVER & SILVERPLATE
VANITY & TABLE ITEMS

For Listing & Pricing See Pages 124-125

132

VICTORIAN & ART NOUVEAU
SILVER TABLE ITEMS

STERLING—STERLING & CRYSTAL
Art Nouveau & Victorian

Courtesy: FLASHBACK ANTIQUE, 489 3rd Ave., N.Y.C. 10016

SILVER & SILVERPLATE TABLE ITEMS
For Listing & Pricing See Page 126

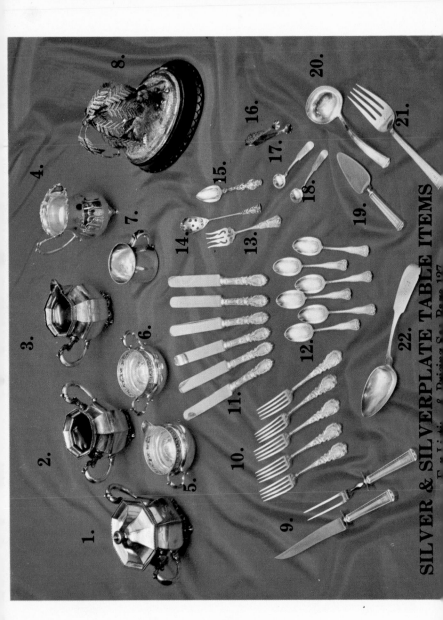

SILVER & SILVERPLATE TABLE ITEMS

For Listings & Pricing See Page 137

DESK SETS—INKSTANDS—DESK FURNISHINGS

The Inkstand had its beginnings in Colonial America. Sterling silver canoe-shaped inkstands, holding cut glass ink bottles on low legs of the 1790's were superseded by oblong trays of the early 1800's with gadrooned rims, holding cut glass bottles. The Victorian inkstand and Desk sets featured rococo piercing, casting and engraving of the most elaborate type, sitting on low floral feet, and made in fanciful designs with animal figures, birds, and classic human figures. Inkstands in combinations of pottery and silver, wood and silver, and glass and silver deposit were made.

The Victorian Inkstands, or Inkwells, held one or two glass bottles with Sterling Silver or Silverplated hinged tops. Desk sets with open trays, or holders, calendars, stamp boxes, pen wipers, and blotters, were produced in a large variety of designs. Art Nouveau Inkstands in Sterling Silver were produced in various floral and sea-motif, mermaids, exotic fish, sea-wave, nude figures, cherubs, flowing haired ladies, etc., by Gorham in Martele silver. These Inkstands, some with candle holders, are among the most beautiful and valuable ever created. The Unger Brothers of Newark also produced unusual Sterling Silver Art Nouveau Inkstands.

*Retail
Silverplate & Crystal
2 Bottles & Tray
$30.00-$70.00

CIRCA 1870

*Silver
$50.00-$150.00

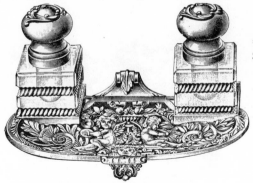

Ink Stand.

*Prices Depend on Design, Size & Condition

DESK SETS—INKSTANDS

Desk Set   Retail $185.00

Retail
Silverplate
& Crystal
$50.00

CIRCA
1870

Ink Stand.

DESK SETS—INKSTANDS

Martelé Silver & Crystal—Retail—**$250.00**
ART NOUVEAU—CIRCA 1895

ART NOUVEAU
CIRCA 1895

Martelé
Silver
Inkstand
With
Candleholder
$200.00

DESK SETS

All Prices
Quoted Are For
Silverplate

Silver Prices
Double

Retail $35.00

Retail $50.00

Retail $65.00

INK BOTTLES AND INKWELLS

A large selection of individual ink bottles in cut, pressed, and etched glass, with Silver and Silverplate hinged tops were produced in the 1880's - 1920's. The tops are in Victorian, Rococo, or Art Nouveau designs. Many can still be found in Antique shops at reasonable prices.

INKWELLS

Sterling Silver Inkwells with glass inserts and no tops in Art Nouveau cylinders were made by most manufacturers. Unger Brothers of Newark produced fine examples of this item in various designs.

Retail
Silverplate & Crystal
Single Bottle & Stand
$20.00-$75.00
Price Depends on Design

ART
NOUVEAU
CIRCA 1895

Martelé
Silver &
Crystal
Inkbottle
& Tray
$175.00

INK BOTTLES & INKWELLS

ART
NOUVEAU
CIRCA 1895

Martelé
Silver &
Crystal
Inkbottle
$75.00

$35.00

$35.00

Retail
Silverplate
& Crystal

$20.00-$75.00

Ink Stand

Ink Stand
$20.00

Ink Stand
$40.00

INK BOTTLES & INKWELLS

*Retail
Silverplate
& Crystal
$20.00-$75.00

$40.00

$65.00

All Prices
For Fine
Condition

$75.00

$35.00

Silver
With
Crystal
Insert
$25.00

*Silver Prices Double.

DESK FURNISHINGS

These include stamp boxes, paper knives, letter openers, calenders, erasers, pen holders, letter clips, pen trays, racks, blotters, pen wipers, seals, book marks, paper shears, glue pots, etc. were all subject to the attention of the Victorian and Art Nouveau designers of Silver and Silverplate. Embossing, engraving, chasing covered all exposed surfaces. Stamp boxes are sometimes mistaken for hairpin boxes. To distinguish between them: The Stamp box has a rounded bottom, the hairpin box is flat.

*Retail
Silverplate—$7.50-$20.00
Silver—$15.00-$40.00
*Price Depends On Design

Blotter

Stamp Box

Thermometer

Letter File

Stamp and Pen Tray

DESK FURNISHINGS
PAPER KNIVES

Sterling,
Martele
$40.00
Each

Silver
Art
Nouveau
1904
$85.00

Silver
Handle
$45.00

DESK FURNISHINGS
THERMOMETER, CALENDARS, BLOTTERS

Silverplate—$7.50-$20.00
Sterling Silver—$10.00-$40.00

SP
$15.00

SS
$30.00

Calendar

SP
$12.50
SS
$25.00

SP
$12.50

SS
$25.00

Stationery Holder and Calendar

Blotter and Calendar Combined.

SP
$10.00

SS
$20.00

SP
$12.50

SS
$25.00

Thermometer

Daily Calendar

SP—Silverplate   SS—Sterling Silver

DESK FURNISHINGS
STERLING SILVER BOOK MARKS

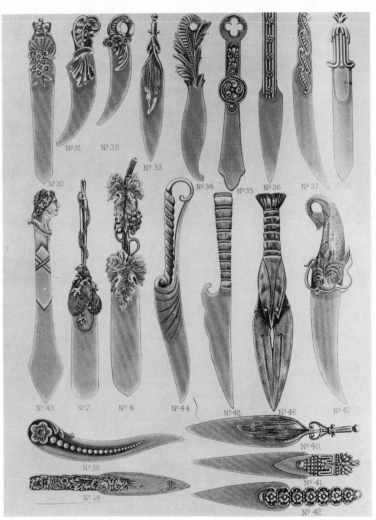

Sterling Silver Book Marks   Retail **$10.00—$15.00**

DESK FURNISHINGS
CUT GLASS INKWELLS—SILVER TOPS

*Silver Tops & Cut Crystal Bottles—$22.50-$45.00

LETTER CLIPS—SILVER

Retail—$10.00—$20.00

*Price Depends on Size of Bottle

DESK FURNISHINGS
SILVER PEN, PENCIL, ERASERS

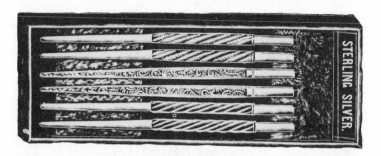

PEN HOLDERS

Each
Retail

Sterling
Silver
$15.00—$25.00

Price Depends
On Design

ERASERS   Silver $8.50

Art Nouveau   Sterling Silver—$30.00

PEN RACK

GENTLEMEN'S ACCESSORIES

Although ladies vanity and toilet accessories were the greatest subject of Silver and Silverplate products, the gentlemen of 1860—1915 were not neglected. Shaving items such as: Shaving mugs, cups, and brushes (fixed and folding), soap boxes, silver and silverplate mounted razor strops, razors with Silver and Silverplate handles were available. Shoe horns and whisk brooms and collar-button boxes, pocket knives, and pocket flasks, canes, and umbrella heads, watches and watch fobs all were designed and embellished in the height of Victorian and Art Nouveau fashion.

SHAVING BRUSHES

The brush handles of Silver and Silverplate were heavily embossed, engraved, and chased in a large variety of designs, Victorian, Rococo, and Art Nouveau. Folding brushes enabled the bristles to recess into the hollow handles for travelling. Due to deteriation brushes complete with original bristles are hard to find.

SHAVING MUGS AND CUPS

Single-handled cups and mugs were used along with shaving soap and brushes to create lather for shaving. Handles and bodies were highly decorated, and the owner's name often engraved. Matching mugs and brushes in Sterling Silver were made from 1880-1915 and are most sought-after and valuable. Complete Shaving Sets with tilting mirror mug, and stand containing a drawer for razor are also rare and valuable in complete, original condition.

GENTLEMEN'S ACCESSORIES
SHAVING BRUSHES

ART NOUVEAU
CIRCA 1904

SP-$20.00

*Sterling Silver—$20.00-$40.00

SHAVING MUGS & CUPS

Silverplate—$50.00
Sterling Silver—$80.00

Shaving Mug and Brush   *Price Depends on Design & Condition

GENTLEMEN'S ACCESSORIES
SHAVING MUGS & CUPS & SETS

Silverplate Set
$125.00 Retail

Retail
Silverplate—$20.00
Sterling Silver—$40.00

SHAVING SET
WITH DRAWER FOR RAZOR

Set—Shaving Mug & Brush

Retail
Silverplate—$40.00
Sterling Silver—$80.00

All Prices for Original Items—Fine Condition

GENTLEMEN'S ACCESSORIES
RAZORS

The gentleman's shaving razor of Victorian times (1840-1900) was an object of much embellishment. Sterling Silver Sheffield plate, and Silverplate were combined with ivory, horn, tortoiseshell, mother of pearl, etc., and embossed, engraved and inlaid into an enormous variety of designs. Art Nouveau razors reflected the flowing and floral designs of the period.

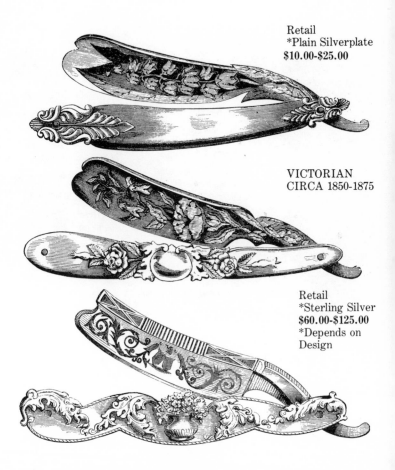

Retail
*Plain Silverplate
$10.00-$25.00

VICTORIAN
CIRCA 1850-1875

Retail
*Sterling Silver
$60.00-$125.00
*Depends on
Design

GENTLEMEN'S ACCESSORIES
SOAP BOXES, SHAVE STICKS, RAZOR STROPS, RAZORS

Silver and Silverplate accessories connected with shaving were numerous. Round and square covered boxes for holding shave soap, shave stick boxes, tube shaped with covers for travelling, all decorated in the Victorian and Art Nouveau fashion.

Leather razor strops were made in Silver and Silverplated mountings with designs typical of Victorian and Rococo influence.

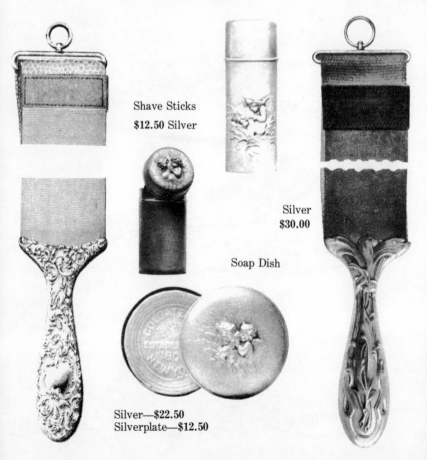

Shave Sticks
$12.50 Silver

Silver
$30.00

Soap Dish

Silver—$22.50
Silverplate—$12.50

GENTLEMEN'S ACCESSORIES
CANES, WALKING STICKS, UMBRELLA HEADS

By the late 1800's most American gentlemen carried silver or gilt-headed canes. Many Silver and Silverplate firms made these masculine status symbols and it was not uncommon for the Victorian man to own several. The "mushroom cap" engraved, etched, and embossed with scrolls and strapwork and top space for a monogram was the most popular type.

These were made in straight cap, round cap, octagon cap, etc. Also popular were the "L" shaped square crook, curve crook, polo crook and the "C" shaped fancy crook.

Canes with heads of silver deposit, combined with Ivory staghorn, and other materials are rare and quite valuable.

These same cane and walking stick handles (crooks) were used on umbrellas as well.

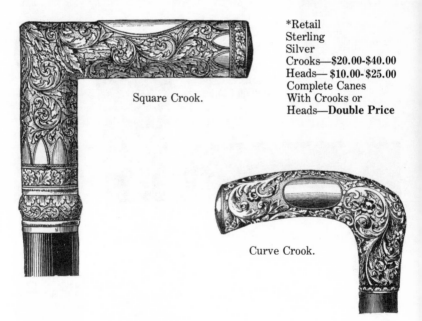

Square Crook.

Curve Crook.

*Retail
Sterling
Silver
Crooks—$20.00-$40.00
Heads— $10.00- $25.00
Complete Canes
With Crooks or
Heads—**Double Price**

*Value Depends on size & design

155

GENTLEMEN'S ACCESSORIES
CANES, WALKING STICKS, UMBRELLA HEADS

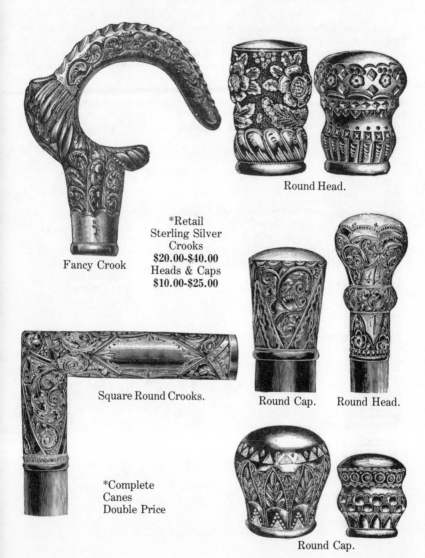

Round Head.

Fancy Crook

*Retail
Sterling Silver
Crooks
$20.00-$40.00
Heads & Caps
$10.00-$25.00

Square Round Crooks.

Round Cap.   Round Head.

*Complete
Canes
Double Price

Round Cap.

GENTLEMEN'S ACCESSORIES
POCKET FLASKS

Silver and Silverplated pocket flasks were among the articles made for gentlemen from the 1800's thru the 1920's. In general they were simple oval shapes "pumpkin seed" with screw-top closings. Prohibition "hip-flasks" were curved to fit the back pocket.

They were often made as mementoes to commemorate a patriotic or festive occasion with embossed or engraved designs illustrating the event.

The Art Nouveau period (1895-1910) produced many examples with typical designs of sinuous females embossed on the flasks.

*Retail

Sterling Silver
& Cut Crystal
$50.00-$80.00

*Price Depends
On Size of Flask
& Designer
Glass Bottle

ART
NOUVEAU
CIRCA 1904

*Retail

Sterling
Silver
$35.00-$75.00

Silverplate
$20.00-$50.00

GENTLEMEN'S ACCESSORIES
DRESS ITEMS

Sterling Silver and silverplate shoe horns, button hooks, whisk brooms and collar-button boxes were an important part of the Victorian man's personal and dress accoutrements. The prevailing whimsy of the period showed in a collar button box in the round shape of an embossed collar and bow with the word "collar" engraved and a button as the cover handle.

A silverplate whisk broom with a liquor flask in the handle has the legend "JUST A FEW" and three birds in flight (swallows) engraved on the body.

Cuff links in all styles and designs in Sterling and Silverplate were worn in the late 1800's. Many examples are to be found today in Antique shops and Flea Markets.

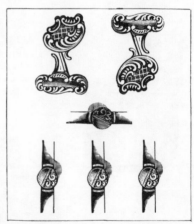

Button Box

Silverplate
$15.00
Silver
$22.50

Retail
Silver—Sets
$20.00
Cuff Links
$10.00-$15.00

158

GENTLEMEN'S ACCESSORIES
DRESS ITEMS

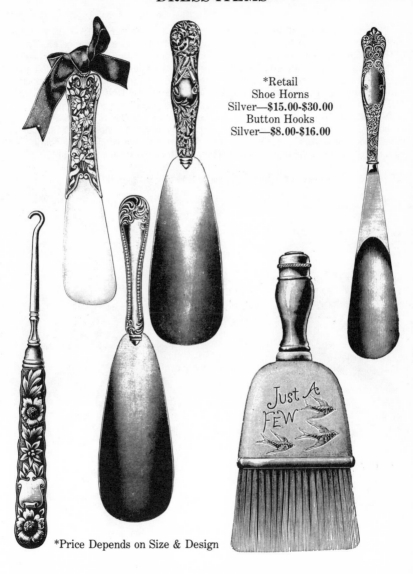

*Retail
Shoe Horns
Silver—$15.00-$30.00
Button Hooks
Silver—$8.00-$16.00

Just A FEW

*Price Depends on Size & Design

GENTLEMEN'S ACCESSORIES
POCKET WATCHES

While the majority of pocket watches produced in the period 1865-1910, were made with gold or gold-filled cases, silver and silverplate were not neglected. Many of the designs made in gold were duplicated in either sterling silver or silverplate.

A special group of silver cases were produced with popular themes etched and engraved on the backs of open-face watches. Illustrations of typical American subjects such as: LOCOMOTIVE, STEAMBOAT, FIRE ENGINES, HORSES, INDIANS, etc. appeared on many watches. Inlays of gold and gold plating created a "two-color" effect on many of these. Hunting case watches (with covers) featuring embossed and chased designs are rising rapidly in value. Those with matching silver link chains are especially desirable. As with gold watches, chronographs in silver are the most valuable in the pocket watch category of collectibles.

All prices quoted are for original pieces in fine working condition.

*Retail
Silver Cases
Plain—$20.00-$50.00
Silver Cases
Engraved Backs
65.00-125.00

$125.00

$75.00

"Locomotive"

*Price
Depends On
Size & Design

"Horseman"

GENTLEMEN'S ACCESSORIES
POCKET WATCHES

Silver, Open Face
Chronograph—$200.00

$85.00

"Steamboat"

*Retail Each

Silver Cases
Plain $20.00-$50.00

Silver Cases
Engraved Backs
$65.00-$125.00

"King of the Forest"

All Prices
For Watches
In Fine
Working
Condition

"Fire Engine"

GENTLEMEN'S ACCESSORIES
SILVER VEST CHAINS

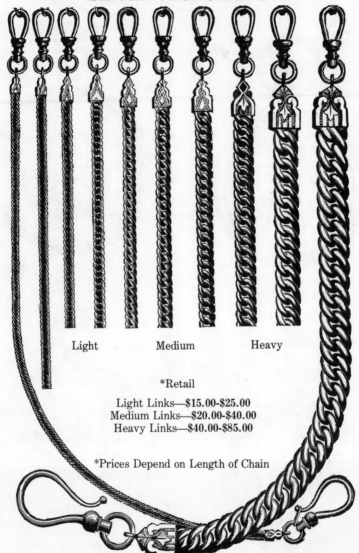

Light   Medium   Heavy

*Retail

Light Links—$15.00-$25.00
Medium Links—$20.00-$40.00
Heavy Links—$40.00-$85.00

*Prices Depend on Length of Chain

LADIES' ITEMS—CHATELAINES
BUCKLES—COMBS—PINS

The American Silversmiths turned their attention to the production of practical and decorative items for ladies of the Victorian and Art Nouveau eras. Purses, pins of all types, pin holders, chatelaines, buckles, clasps, veil holders, combs, glove hooks, opera glasses, Vinaigrettes and glove colognes, etc.

Design motifs used on these feminine pieces ranged from Victorian rococo thru Art Nouveau with the emphasis on flowery forms, cherubs and nymphs, ladies heads with flowing tresses and birds of every type at rest and in flight. Many of these feminine artifacts are to be found in quantity antique shops, flea markets and other sources.

CHATELAINES

Dating back to earliest history the chatelaine was a decorative and practical small flat plate with a flat hook that fitted into the waistband and had three or more chains suspended, holding a watch, smelling salts bottle, a pair of spectacles, etc., or a "sewing" chatelaine with scissors, pincushions, needle-holders, etc., or a "religious" chatelaine with church items on the chains. The plates in silver and silverplate appeared in every variety of Victorian rococo and Art Nouveau design.

AMERICAN CHATELAINE WATCHES

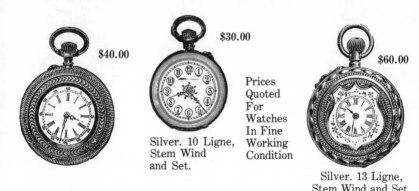

$40.00

$30.00

Silver. 10 Ligne, Stem Wind and Set.

Prices Quoted For Watches In Fine Working Condition

$60.00

Silver. 13 Ligne, Stem Wind and Set.

LADIES ITEMS—CHATELAINES

*Retail
Silver—$20.00-$50.00
Silverplate—$10.00-$20.00

*Price Depends On Size,
& Number of Chains, Design

Chatelaines
With
Stones
Worth
More

CIRCA
1865-1895

LADIES ITEMS
GLOVE COLOGNES

VINAIGRETTE—SALTS BOTTLE

*Prices Depend on Size & Design

*Retail
Silver & Cut Crystal
$15.00-$40.00 Each

LADIES ITEMS
BUCKLES & PINS

In the late 1800's and early 1900's, belt buckles, girdle buckles, cloak clasps, and pins of all types were produced in an enormous variety of designs with Victorian, Rococo, and Art Nouveau dominating. Silversmiths like Unger Bros. of Newark made pin and buckle Art Nouveau designs of women's heads and figures with flowing hair and drapery.

Hair pins, hat pins, lace pins were produced in every Victorian motif and concept. Birds, animals, swords, flowers, etc. were made in Sterling Silver and often gold plated or set with semi-precious stones.

*Retail

Pins	Buckles
Silverplate—$8.50-$20.00	$12.50-$35.00
Sterling Silver—$12.50-$50.00	$25.00-$85.00

*Prices Depend
On Design,
Condition &
Weight of
Silver
in Buckles

ART NOUVEAU
CIRCA 1900

*Art Nouveau Pieces
In Silver are Most Valuable

ROCOCO-CIRCA 1880
VICTORIAN

LADIES ITEMS
SCABBARD PINS

*Retail
Silverplate—$7.50-$20.00
Silver—$10.00-$30.00

Silver
$15.00

Silver
$30.00

Silver
$18.50

Silver $20.00

Pins With Stones
Worth More.
Diamond &
Silver
$75.00

LADIES ITEMS—HAT PINS

NO. 126   NO. 127   128

Veil Holder.

*Retail
Silver Plate
$5.00-$12.50
Silver
$8.50-$20.00

*Price depends on design.

168

LADIES ITEMS
COMBS—PURSES

Silver decorative combs with open fretwork designs were popular in the 1880's. Mesh purses of silver and silverplate were carried for evening wear. The heavy frames were usually embellished in Victorian designs, and often the purses were suspended from chains.

*Retail
Sterling Silver
$30.00-$100.00
*Depending on Size
& Design

CIRCA
1890

Silverplate
$15.00-$50.00

LADIES ITEMS
PURSES

Sterling
Silver
$40.00

Purse.

Sterling
Silver
$60.00

Purse.

Sterling
Silver
$75.00

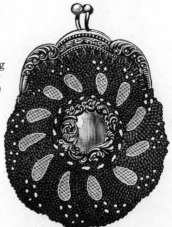

*Retail
Silverplate—$25.00-$50.00
Silver—$35.00-$125.00

*Price Depend on Size,
Design & Condition

Purse.

LAMPS

From 1850 to 1900 kerosene lamps were advertised and sold by many silver and silverplate manufacturers. The body and base of the lamp were usually decorated in Victorian designs that frequently reached a height of elaborate embellishment. The shades were often Cut Glass such as: Amber, Rubina Verde, Mary Gregory, etc., decorated with enameled and etched designs.

Gorham Mfg. Co. made Art Nouveau lamps in Sterling Silver embossed and chased with nymphs and flower forms.

Complete lamps with the original glass shades are very rare and valuable, due to breakage and collectability by Cut Glass enthusiasts.

*Price Depends on Size & Condition & Glass Shade.

LAVATORY SETS

Although china and porcelain were the principal materials used in making these wash table items, many Silver & Silverplate manufacturers produced Ewer and Basin sponge dishes, soap boxes, tooth brush boxes and holders in a variety of designs and styles. The Art Nouveau products of silver are the most valuable and collectable.

LAVATORY SETS

*Retail
Silverplate—$20.00-$25.00
Silver—$30.00-$200.00

Tooth Brush Box—$35.00

Sponge Bowl—$20.00

Cup—$20.00

Soap Box—$30.00

$125.00-$250.00

*Price Depends
On Design & Weight
Or Silver

LAVATORY SETS

Martelé Art Nouveau Complete Set **$1200.00**
Sterling Silver
CIRCA 1904

Silverplate Art Nouveau
CIRCA 1900

Set **$250.00**

PRIZE CUPS & AWARDS

In America of the 1700's & 1800's, loving cups, prize cups, and awards were an important feature of ceremonies, presentations, and prize giving. Among the most beautiful and valuable single items of silver ever produced were mementoes of gratitude presented to victors in Americas' battles by cities, states, and private citizens. The most popular shapes for these awards were urns, vases, and bowl form centerpieces. The most elaborate molding, engraving, chasing, and repousse figures and themes covered the surface. Most of the important pieces are in museums and institutions.

Prize cups and awards (circa 1860-1910) for popular use were produced by all American silver and silverplate manufacturers. Subject matter such as sports, scholastic awards, business achievements, etc., were the basis for designs. The elaborate presentation vases, and urns in the Art Nouveau style and rising rapidly in value.

CIRCA 1880

*Retail
Silverplate $65.00-$95.00
Silver $150.00-$350.00

*Retail
Silverplate $85.00-$150.00
Silver
$200.00-$500.00

*Price Depends On
Size Decoration, &
Weight of Silver

PRIZE CUPS & AWARDS

Martelé
Sterling Silver
26" High—CIRCA 1902
Retail $1750.00

Prize
Vases
Martelé

Martelé
Sterling Silver
24" High—CIRCA 1900
Retail $2500.00

SEWING ITEMS

During the Victorian era, needlework was the chief occupation of most women. From childhood onward women were trained in all the sewing skills needed to produce table items, clothing, and decorative needlework of all types.

Silver and Silverplate manufacturers produced a great variety of items to fill this very practical and important need. Among the many products made were: Sewing sets, pin cushions, pin cabinets, spool boxes, needlecases, thimbles, bodkins and ribbon pulls, and scissors of all types.

THIMBLES

Hand made silver thimbles were imported into Colonial America from Europe but by the middle 1700's American silversmiths were making them. By the mid-1800's mechanical production of thimbles was the common procedure. The borders and bands were engraved and embossed with floral motifs, or scenes of ships, houses and country views, windmills, bicycling men.

Many thimbles were made with souvenir subjects such as historic buildings and locations or World's Fair themes. Silver thimbles are readily available in antique shops, etc., and are an easy-to-collect category of Victorian and Art Nouveau.

SEWING ITEMS

Thimbles

$6.00—$15.00
Prices Depend On Design

Pincushion
$15.00

PINCUSHIONS
$8.00-$20.00

Prices
Depend
On
Design

Pincushion

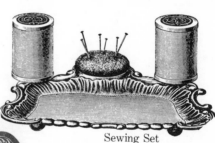

Sewing Set

Pincushion

Complete Set
$75.00

Needlecase
$10.00

177

SEWING ITEMS

PIN CUSHIONS

Victorian design manifested itself in the great variety of motifs used in these receptacles for needles and pins. Some were made with legs, a miniature Victorian chair for example some sat on embossed bases. Pin cushions are a desirable group of collectables and are still to be found in many antique shops and flea markets.

SEWING BIRDS

The ladies of the 1850's to 1880's had these useful and decorative clamps to assist them in doing needlework. Made in the shape of a bird, they were fixed to the edge of a table. The beak could be opened to hold any fabric or material to be sewn. The bird carried a pin cushion on his back and one on the clamp.

Retail
Silverplate
$20.00

Sterling
Silver
$35.00

SCISSORS

All silver manufacturing companies made small sewing scissors and scissors for other purposes, such as grape scissors, poultry scissors, desk scissors, etc.

German and English steel mills usually provided the blades. The Sterling Silver handles were usually decorated in the Rococo Victorian style of scrolls and floral motifs. Unusual handles were also made, such as; grape scissors with grape and leaf design handles, stork shaped sewing scissors with the blades forming the beak, and other figural handles such as dog and hunter, double dolphin, witch of Salem, etc.

Scissors collecting is a good area for collecting interesting and potentially valuable Victorian silver artifacts.

*Retail
Silverplate
$12.50—$25.00
Sterling Silver
$22.50—$60.00

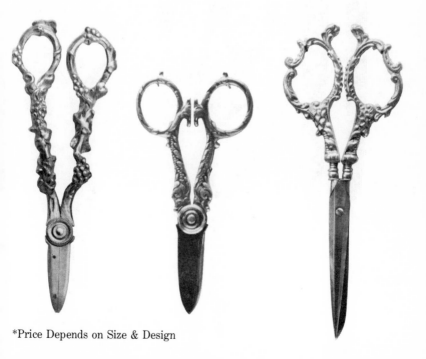

*Price Depends on Size & Design

SCISSORS

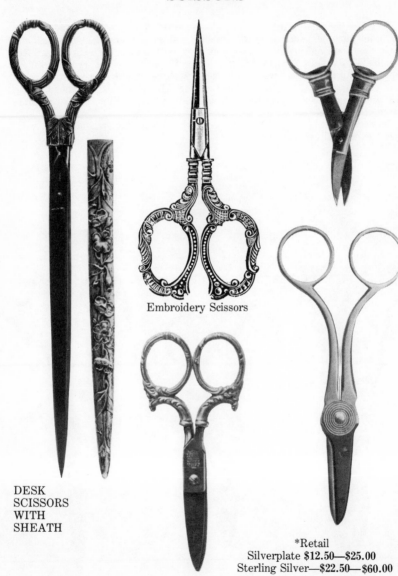

Embroidery Scissors

DESK
SCISSORS
WITH
SHEATH

*Retail
Silverplate $12.50—$25.00
Sterling Silver—$22.50—$60.00

VASES & EWERS

The Victorian love of flowers and the art of bouquet-making found their proper outlets in the myriad varieties of vases produced by the Silver and Silverplate Manufacturers of America. By the 1870's elaborate ornate vases and bud vases decorated in every imaginable style were advertised and sold. Classic figurines and others proliferated: Apollo, Gladiator, Egyptian Queens and Pharoahs, Indian Chief and Squaw, Chinese Mandarin, Victorian Lady with Flower Basket, animals and birds such as deer, dogs, foxes, lions, peacocks, pheasants, canaries, cats, etc. all were either decorated on the vase, or cast as figurals on the frames and bases.

Beautiful cut glass vases on silver and silverplated mounts have been sought by glass collectors, and are quite rare and expensive. The glass vases were engraved, pressed, cut, enamelled, and decorated in every sentimental style and fashion of the Victorian era.

Peachblow, Amberina, Rubina Verde, Mary Gregory, Agata, Burmese, Amethyst, Ruby, etc. were among the types of highly desirable cut glass employed in Vases and Bud Vases.

Pottery was also used, though less frequently, in Silver & Silverplate mounts. The Gorham Silver Company combined elaborate pierced frames and silver overlay with Rookwood pottery vases. Rookwood pottery was Art pottery made at Cincinnati by Mrs. Mabel Bellamy Storer, and other artists, circa 1880.

The pieces were often signed by the artist and always marked with the "RP" symbol and flames. Gorham also made the individual Martele vases in Sterling Silver with Art Nouveau floral embossed shapes and motifs.

The Rookwood and Silver overlay Vases, and the Martele pieces are very valuable and among the finest examples of the Silversmiths art.

VASES & EWERS

Silverplate
VICTORIAN
CIRCA 1865-1880

*Retail
$50.00-$150.00

*Prices Depend On
Type of Glass
Vase Insert

VASES & EWERS

MARTELÉ

ART NOUVEAU
CIRCA 1895—1905

Sterling
Silver
$60.00-$175.00
Depending On
Size & Design

Rookwood
Vase &
Silver
Overlay
CIRCA 1901
$225.00

VASES & EWERS

These were large wide mouthed water pitchers with handles originally made in the middle ages through the 1700's. Along with the matching bowl, they were used by nobles of the times to wash their hands in a ceremonial manner. The water, often rose scented, was poured over the hands into the basin.

The helmet shape of the ewer with a curved spout and an "S" shaped handle often in the form of a sinuous female figure was made during the Art Nouveau period. The Gorham Sterling Martelé Ewers and plateau are fine examples of these items, with embossed, repousse and chased figures and wave forms, Rockwood pottery vases encased in Art Nouveau Sterling fretwork, were also made by Gorham, and are quite scarce and valuable.

ART
NOUVEAU

CIRCA 1901

Rookwood
Ewer
& Silver
Overlay

12" High

Retail
$200.00
Each

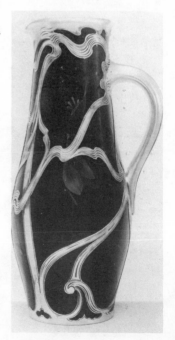

184

VASES & EWERS

ART
NOUVEAU
CIRCA
1904
Silver
$65.00

Rookwood
Vase &
Silver
Overlay
300.00

STERLING SILVER VANITY ITEMS

Item, description	Retail
1. Art nouveau sterling silver calling card tray	$210.00
2. Sterling Silver Vanity table box	$45.00
3. Art nouveau sterling silver picture frame	$45.00
4. Sterling silver pin cushion	$20-35.00
5. 10. & 11. One sterling silver set, hand mirror, 2 brushes, very high relief, made in China for the European market	Set $250.00
6. Art nouveau sterling silver pin tray	$20-35.00
7a. Magnifying glass, converted sterling silver handle	$15-30.00
7b. Beaded purse, sterling silver art nouveau motif top	$30-50.00
8a. Art nouveau, sterling silver figural seal	$30.00
8b. Art nouveau, sterling silver seal, set with rubies	$50.00
9. Silver plated jewel box	$14-45.00
9a. Art nouveau sterling silver desk thermometer	$35.00
10. See No. 5.	
11. See No. 5.	
12. Art nouveau sterling silver seal figural	$30.00
13. 14. 15. 16. 17. & 27. One sterling silver art nouveau set: nail file, hand mirror, nail pick, clothes brush, shoe horn, comb	Complete set $180.00 single pieces, range $5-35.00
18. Sterling silver art nouveau pocket wallet, leather lined with ivory memo page; rare	$135.00
19. Silver plated jewel box	$15-45.00
20. Art nouveau sterling silver button hook	$20-45.00
21. Art nouveau sterling silver glove stretcher	$20-45.00
22. Sterling silver cane top; carved Indian chief	$40.00
23. Sterling silver "Tiffany" hallmark, shoe horn	$45.00
24. Sterling silver art nouveau button hook	$20-45.00
25. Sterling silver art nouveau travel soap dish	$30-45.00
26. Sterling silver art nouveau pocket mirror	$25.00
27. See No. 13.	
28. & 29. Sterling silver art nouveau button hook	$25.00 each
30. Sterling silver art nouveau handle sock darner	$27.00
31. Quadruple plate table box	$18.00
32. Sterling silver hand mirror, floral embossing	$45.00
33. Signed and dated etched sterling silver snuff box; American hallmark	$100.00

STERLING SILVER VANITY ITEMS

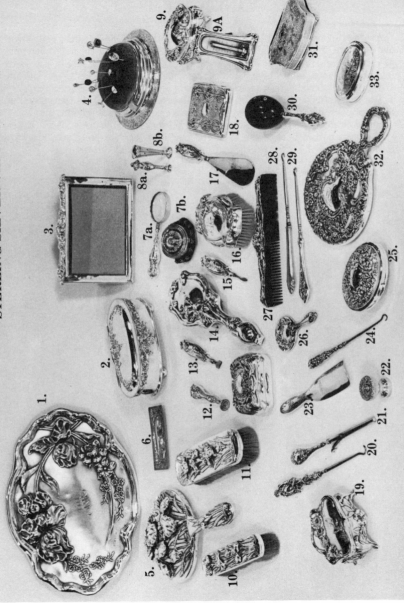

VANITY ITEMS

Among the most desirable, valuable, and collectable items of Silver and Silver-plate are the dresser appointments and vanity items made for the ladies boudoirs of Victorian and pre-World War I America. Although individual pieces, especially mirrors, brushes, and sets are known from earlier times it wasn't until the late 1880's that matched sets appeared in many manufacturers' catalogs.

The Art Nouveau style of 1890—1910 in dresser and vanity sets were plentiful, the sets consisted of hand mirror, hair-brush, combs, whisk broom, and some-times were made with matching nail file, tooth brush, manicure scissors, cuticle knife, shoe button hook, shoe horn and curling iron. Complete sets are hard to find, and are the most valuable of this category of collectibles.

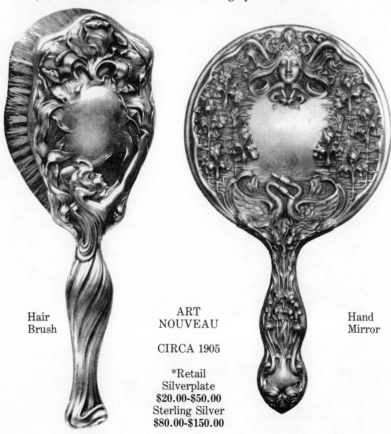

Hair
Brush

ART
NOUVEAU

CIRCA 1905

*Retail
Silverplate
$20.00-$50.00
Sterling Silver
$80.00-$150.00

Hand
Mirror

VANITY ITEMS—DRESSER SETS

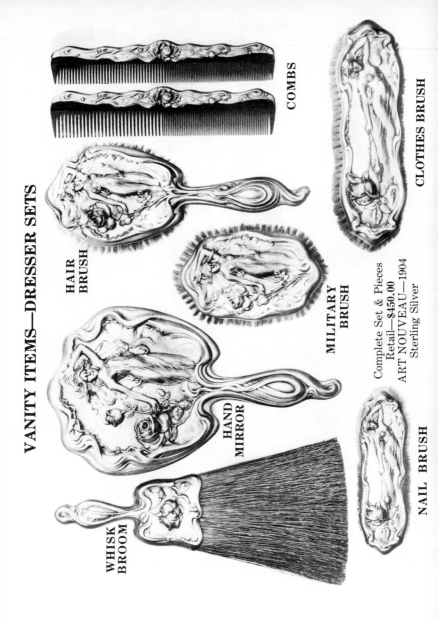

COMBS

CLOTHES BRUSH

HAIR BRUSH

MILITARY BRUSH

Complete Set & Pieces
Retail—$450.00
ART NOUVEAU—1904
Sterling Silver

HAND MIRROR

NAIL BRUSH

WHISK BROOM

189

VANITY ITEMS—DRESSER SETS

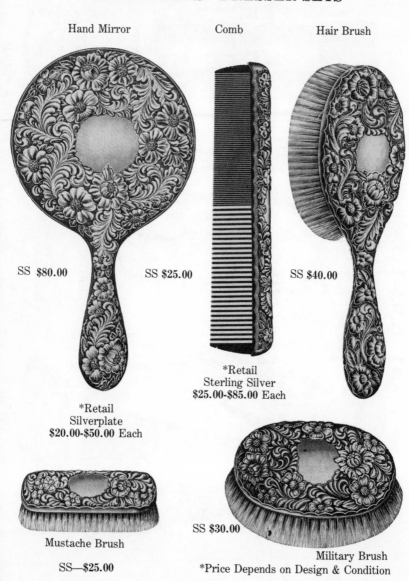

Hand Mirror

Comb

Hair Brush

SS $80.00

SS $25.00

SS $40.00

*Retail
Sterling Silver
$25.00-$85.00 Each

*Retail
Silverplate
$20.00-$50.00 Each

SS $30.00

Mustache Brush

SS—$25.00

Military Brush
*Price Depends on Design & Condition

VANITY ITEMS—DRESSER SETS

COMPLETE SETS
IN THE SAME
PATTERN

Silver
$150.00-$350.00
Silverplate
$80.00-$175.00
Sets Are Rare

SS
$28.50

SS
$30.00

BONNET BRUSH

WHISK BROOM

SS—$20.00

HAT BRUSH

SS—$30.00

VELVET BRUSH

*Retail
Sterling Silver
$25.00-$65.00
Silverplate
$20.00-$50.00

VANITY ITEMS—MANICURE SETS

Manicure sets were made in a great variety of designs around the early 1900's. Cuticle scissors and knives, nail files, polishers, corn knives, cream boxes, etc. often on a matching tray or in a fitted box. Art Nouveau motifs of flowing hair ladies and nudes, cherubs and flowers, sinuous items and leaves and asymmetrical curves were ideally suited to personal vanity items, and many handles and bodies were cast and chased in these forms.

Complete sets are difficult to find, but individual items are available at Antique Shops, auctions, flea markets, etc.

Individual Pieces in Sterling Silver made by Gorham Mfg. Co., and by Unger Brothers of Newark, N.J., are true and valued examples of the height of the Art Nouveau Silversmiths craft.

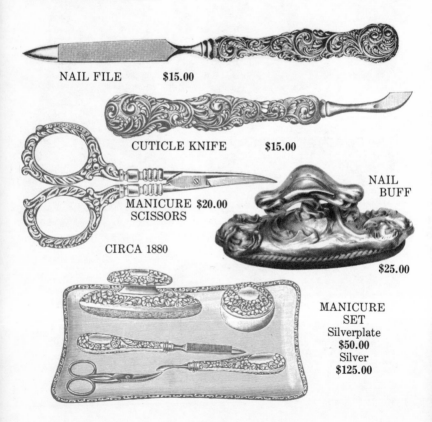

NAIL FILE $15.00

CUTICLE KNIFE $15.00

MANICURE $20.00
SCISSORS

CIRCA 1880

NAIL
BUFF

$25.00

MANICURE
SET
Silverplate
$50.00
Silver
$125.00

VANITY ITEMS—TOILET STANDS

Important features of the Victorian ladies boudoir dressing table were these combinations of cologne and perfume bottles, and powder puff boxes in decorative cut glass of all types in pink, blue, yellow, green, opaque and translucent colors.

Butterflies, birds, flowers, children playing (in "Mary Gregory" style) where used as decorative themes on the glass.

The stands, made of Silverplate and often gold decorated, were as elaborate as Victorian manufacturers could make them, with Egyptian, Rococo, and Classic figures and embellishments. The stands usually held three bottles, but were also known with one or two bottles and rarely, three bottles and a bud vase.

Although made in great numbers and variety during the period of 1800—1900, Toilet Stands are quite scarce today due to the breakage of the bottles, and their desireability to Art Glass collectors.

*Retail
Silverplate
$30.00-$125.00
*Depending on Size,
Design, No. of Bottles

With Art Glass
Bottles Worth
More

"Mary
Gregory"
Type
Toilet
Stand

Silverplate Single Bottle Type $30.00-$75.00

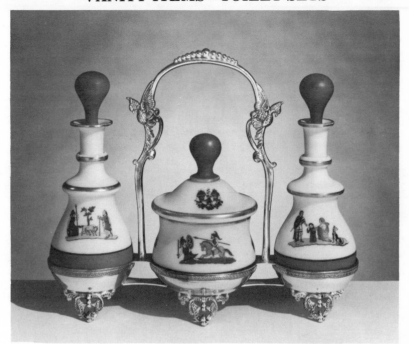

3 Bottle $85.00

3 Bottle
Type $150.00

Single Bottle $65.00

MIRRORS

Plate-glass table mirrors made in the Victorian period are a unique and charming vanity item. Elaborately decorated with birds, flowers, angels, etc., they were made with and without covers as dressing table features, and for the wall with candle sconces. These also are scarce and valuable.

*Retail
Silverplate $50.00-$175.00
Sterling Silver $60.00-$250.00

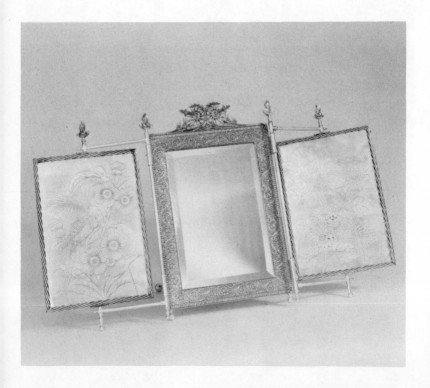

Folding Mirror—Silverplate $150.00

AMERICAN SILVER & SILVERPLATE TABLE ITEMS

TABLE OF CONTENTS

STERLING SILVER AND
SILVER PLATED TABLE ITEMS

Item, description, date   Retail

1a. Sterling silver Georgian sugar tongs $100.00
b. Silver plated "Mappin & Webb" sugar tongs $20.00
c. Sterling silver sugar tongs..................................... $45.00
d. Polish silver plated compote $45.00
2. Silver plated water pitcher; circa 1865 ....$150.00
3. Pair of sterling silver candlesticks; circa 1890 .... $135.00 pr.
4. Sterling silver bud vase $21.00
5. Pair of Gorham sterling silver candlesticks; 1920's .... $125.00 pr.
6. Sterling silver vase; circa 1900's............................. $35.00
6a. Sterling silver rose bell push; circa 1920's. $75.00
7. Sterling silver candelabra, Art Deco.; 1925-1935 .... $135.00
8. Silver plated Victorian sugar bowl with spoon holder $55.00
9. Silver plated Georgian candlestick .... $180.00 pr.
10. "Tiffany & Co." match ashtray................................. $30.00
11. Sterling silver cigarette urn $27.00
12. Sterling silver salt and pepper shakers. .... $29.00 pr.
13. Sterling silver candy dish $30.00
14. Sterling silver cigarette urn $27.00
15. Sterling silver card tray..................................... $35.00
16. Sterling silver compote $35.00
17. & 18. Sterling silver sugar and creamer .... $45.00 set
19. Sterling silver cigarette urn $27.00
20. Sterling silver cigarette urn $25.00
21. Sterling silver match holder and ashtray $39.00
22. Sterling silver shrimp bowl $39.00
23. "Mappin & Webb" plated shell ash tray $15.00
24. Assorted sterling silver napkin rings .... $39.00 (9 pieces)
25. Sterling silver vegetable server $27.00
26. Sterling silver fish serving fork $90.00
27. Chicken shears, sterling silver handles $45.00
28. Art Nouveau cake server, sterling silver handle $35.00
29. Sterling silver petit four server.............................. $27.00
30. Sterling silver souvenir spoon................................. $18.00
31. Sterling silver miniature creamer $18.00
32. Sterling silver cigarette urn $27.00
33. "Mappin & Webb" silver plated salt shaker..................... $10.00
34. Sterling silver baby cup and saucer $35.00
35. Sterling silver salt and pepper shakers .... $29.00 pr.
36. Set of four sterling silver salt cellars $65.00
                                        (Salt spoons -3- $12.00 each.)
37. & 38. Collectors' item, Queen Mary cobalt lined salts.
39. Sterling silver salt spoon $9.00
40. Authors collection: sterling silver fish salt cellar $45.00

STERLING SILVER AND SILVERPLATE TABLE ITEMS

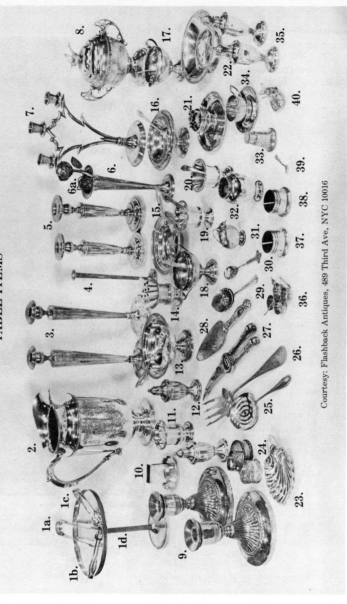

Courtesy: Flashback Antiques, 489 Third Ave, NYC 10016

BAR ITEMS

A great variety of liquor and bar items were produced from 1860-1900 by American silver and silverplate manufacturers in both sterling silver and silverplate. Corkscrews, muddlers, liquor labels, wine funnels, bar jiggers, bar strainers, glass holders, beer pitchers, hot whiskey pitchers, etc., were made in large quantities and in many designs.

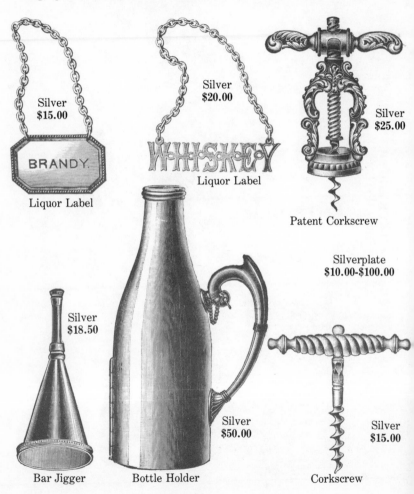

Silver
$15.00

BRANDY.

Liquor Label

Silver
$20.00

WHISKEY

Liquor Label

Silver
$25.00

Patent Corkscrew

Silverplate
$10.00-$100.00

Silver
$18.50

Bar Jigger

Silver
$50.00

Bottle Holder

Silver
$15.00

Corkscrew

200

BAKING DISHES

Inside the baking dish was a porcelain liner in which the item to be baked was placed; this only went into the oven. To serve, the liner was placed on the sterling, or silver plated, receptacle.

The baking dish is found with, and without the cover. The most valuable are those complete with original porcelain liners and covers.

*Retail
Silverplate $50.00-$150.00
Sterling Silver $150.00-$300.00

*Depending on Size, Design
Condition and Weight of Silver

VICTORIAN
CIRCA 1880

BAKING DISHES

*Retail
Silverplate $50.00-$150.00
Sterling Silver $150.00-$300.00

*Depending
On Size, Design,
Condition
& Weight
Of Silver

VICTORIAN
CIRCA 1880

BON-BON BASKETS

Bon-bon dishes and baskets were used to serve chocolates and sweets in the late 1890's. The dishes were produced in both sterling silver and silverplate. They were made with elaborate embossed borders, often pierced. Bon-bon baskets featured a variety of embossed, engraved and chased styles, with bail handles, and sometimes with tongs. They are known both footed and flat.

Unger Bros. Silversmith factory of Newark, N.J., made bon-bon dishes in sterling silver in Art Nouveau motifs featuring flowing-haired women and flowers, blossoms, and leaves. These pieces are most desirable and valuable.

Silverplate $30.00—$80.00
*Silver $60.00-$150.00

*Depends on Size & Weight of Silver

BUTTER DISHES

To understand the need for these practical items, one must know that most butter was made at home on the farm. The extra butter produced on farms was sold to the closest market or store in one pound round cup-shaped molds, imprinted with "hallmark" of the housewife in the form of a butter "print."

Butter dishes of Britannia metal were made in the 1850's. By the 1880's butter dishes were produced by all silverplate manufacturers in a large variety of designs. Most were made with the same basic shape, a round truncated ball, the top half functioning as a cover that could be raised, or lifted and suspended from a hook in the arched handle, tilted back on hinges, or rolled under the base. The base platform was perforated to allow melted ice to drain. A clip containing a butter knife was often a part of the base. Elaborate birds, floral and baroque Victorian designs were engraved, embossed and chased on the base, legs, and cover. Cow finials were sometimes featured.

The double wall butter dish permitted the ice to be inserted in the space between the outside and inside wall of the dish.

Retail
Silverplate $30.00-$80.00
Price Depends on Size, Design
Condition & Accessories

BUTTER DISHES

Left to right: Butter dish with hanging cover, made by Middletown Plate Co., c. 1885. Two butter dishes with revolving covers—shown open and partly closed—made by the Meriden Britannia Co. between 1882 and 1887.

VICTORIAN CIRCA 1875

With cover open

BREAD & CAKE BASKETS

These practical and attractive table items were introduced during the reign of George II and were made in Sterling Silver in a wide variety of designs and shapes.

About 1770, Sheffield plate baskets were introduced with the swing handle and decorated with piercing, chasing and engraving. They were oblong or oval in shape in imitation of the sterling silver models, and produced in large quantities, in hundreds of designs.

The silverplate baskets copied both the Sterling and Sheffield products. Ornamental handles and borders with grape and leaf, rope, beading, gadrooning, scrolling, and piercing were a feature of baskets of the 1860's. The bodies were engraved and chased in floral and baroque motifs. Classic medallions were often integrated with the overall designs.

By the 1870's and 1880's, cake baskets appeared on four foot, and often heavily decorated tall pedestals. The designs became typical of the period, over-embellished and very elaborate with molded cherubs, classic figures, birds, etc. Some baskets were "squared off" in the style of the 1870's. Surface decoration of these baskets were chased birds, cherubs, flowers, often inlaid with gold plate.

VICTORIAN
CIRCA 1869

*Retail
Silverplate
$85.00-$125.00
Sterling
Silver
$100.00-$250.00

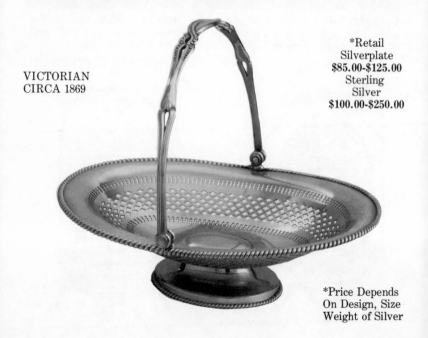

*Price Depends
On Design, Size
Weight of Silver

CAKE BASKETS

VICTORIAN
CIRCA 1870-1890
*Retail
Silverplate
$85.00-$125.00
Silver $100.00-$250.00

*Price
Depends On Size,
Design & Weight
Of Silver

CHAFING DISHES

The chafing dish was known in Old England in the 1500's. Throughout the centuries it evolved to the form it is known today, an inner container for the food, the outer container filled with hot water heated by a burner.

The chafing dishes of the late 1800's were made by many American silverplate manufacturers. They used alcohol burners and stood on either three or four legs. They were made both with and without handles, and were often elaborately decorated in the Victorian or Art Nouveau style. These chafing dishes were heated by alcohol burners. Complete units with stands and burners are the most valuable.

*Retail

Silverplate $75.00-$150.00

Sterling Silver $150.00-$350.00

Chafing Dish. (Nickel Silver.)

*Price
Depends On
Size, Design
Condition

CELERY STANDS

Between 1860 and 1900 these practical table items were very popular for serving celery stalks. The tall silverplate stands were made with a large variety of glass during the 1800's—glass inserts were: pressed, cut crystal, engraved, clear, frosted, and colored glass of all types: Ruby, Amberina, Cranberry, Peachblow, Venetian Thread, Burmese, etc.

The two types of celery holders are, the tall stand on a pedestal, and low rectangular cut glass trays set in footed Silverplate frames. The frames were elaborately decorated in design motifs of the Victorian period.

VICTORIAN
CIRCA 1870-1895

*Retail
Silverplate
$30.00-$100.00
*Price Depends
On Glass.
Art Glass
Most Valuable

COFFEE POTS—CHOCOLATE POTS

While not as popular and widely used as tea pots, many fine examples of silver coffee pots were made in England and Europe from late 1600's to the 1800's. In general the design and shape emulated tea pots of similar times.

American silver and silverplate producers made coffee pots as a part of tea sets and advertised by them as such. The coffee pot was usually very similar in shape and design to the tea pot but was taller.

After dinner coffee pots became a popular individual table item in the late 1880's. They were made in long necked exotic shapes in the fashion of Turkish, Moorish, Persian, and East Indian originals.

After dinner, or black coffee sets, in these motifs were made by Gorham, Wm. Kirk & Son, Reed & Barton, Tiffany & Company and others. The Sterling Silver sets of this period are increasing rapidly in value.

CHARTER OAK
CIRCA 1861

Retail
Silverplate
$50.00-$150.00
Silver
$75.00-$250.00

*Price Depends
On Design &
Condition

COFFEE POTS & URNS

COFFEE URN
CIRCA 1878

*Retail
Silverplate
$80.00-$200.00
Silver
$200.00-$450.00

*Price Depends On
Design & Condition
& Weight of Silver

COFFEE POTS
GORHAM—VICTORIAN CIRCA 1890

No. 040   No. 048

SILVERPLATE—**$50.00**—**$150.00** Each.
Silver **$75.00**—**$150.00** Each.

CREAMERS (MILK JUGS)

The addition of hot milk to tea served in England in early 1700 required an appropriate Silver serving vessel. Hot milk jugs were practical table items with handle and spout on a variety of body shapes: helmet, oval, baluster, octagonal, etc. Many early designs were simple and classic but by the mid 1700's, more elaborate embellishments such as casting and chasing, piercing and scroll-work featuring animal and classic figures appeared. The creamer stood on a single pedestal, three ball feet, or flat on its base, they are known both with and without hinged cover.

By the Victorian period the creamer had been relegated to an adjunct to the serving of tea or coffee and its design was complimentary to the rest of the set. Beading and engraving and applied medallions were popular decorative motifs.

Individual creamers are not nearly as desireable or valuable as complete Sugar and Cream sets.

*Retail
Silverplate **$8.50-$20.00**
Sterling Silver **$20.00-$85.00**

Sugar & Creamer Sets
Silverplate **$20.00-$80.00**
Sterling Silver **$40.00-$130.00**

Prices Depend On Design, Size, Condition & Weight of Silver.

CRYSTAL, SILVER, AND
SILVERPLATE TABLE ITEMS

Item, description, date	Retail

1. 4 pc. cruet set, plated stand and caps,
Baccarrat swirl-pattern glass; circa 1890 .... $50.00
2. 4 pc. cruet set, plated stand and caps,
crystal bottles; circa 1900 .... $45.00
3. Crystal decanter, English; circa 1890 .... $45.00
4. "Mappin & Webb" silver soldered bottle holder;
circa 1890 .... $45.00
5. Etched crystal ewer with plated top and two
matching .table vases; Polish, circa 1890 .... $135.00
6. Plated-base blown crystal vase; Polish,
circa 1880 .... $45.00

7. Two crystal salt cellars on plated base;
English, circa 1890 .... $45-65.00
8. Early maple syrup dispenser (VSA), blown glass,
metal top; circa 1900 .... $50.00
9. Early maple syrup dispenser (VSA), blown glass,
metal top; circa 1900 .... $15.00
10. Desserts or sherberts, sterling base
screw-in etched crystal bowl $90.00
11. Same.
12. Open cheese dish, etched crystal glass,
sterling rim with sterling cutter;
circa 1900 .... $35.00
13. 14. & 15. Crystal salts with condiment bowl,
sterling base, signed "Hawkes." $135.00
16. Blown crystal and sterling tankard; circa 1890 .... $45.00
17. Etched crystal plate with sterling rim; circa 1920 .... $25-35.00
18. Pressed glass cigarette box with sterling rim;
Russian, circa 1920... $120.00
19. Sterling silver and cut crystal sugar caster $15.00
20. Salt and pepper shakers, crystal and sterling silver $15-30.00
21. Sterling silver bibelot $30.00

CRYSTAL, STERLING SILVER & SILVERPLATE TABLE ITEMS

CASTORS

Most tables of the Victorian era were graced with these decorative and practical receptacles for bottle containing spices and condiments. During the 1850's many varieties of the castor were patented including the "Ferris Wheel" type revolving castor.

The essential design of the castor was a Silverplate frame set on short legs or on a taller center pedestal. An ornate wide band circled the container that enclosed the bottles. Six bottles usually fitted in spaces provided. A pierced, or embossed handle rose in the center to be used to pass the castor at the table.

Designs ran riot on the castors of the late 1880's, a bewildering variety of frames and bottles were produced. Engraving, embossing and castings of every style and period were used—Rococo, Greek classic, Victorian and Oriental covered these dining table central pieces. Reed & Barton in the 1870's had a four bottle castor in a cart pulled by a proud peacock. Other manufacturers competed with their own elaborate creations. The 1880's tall revolving castors dominated in hundreds of varieties including four bottles, two bottle, and even one bottle.

Castor bottles were available in every range of glass decor, engraved, etched, cut, pressed, and in combinations of these techniques. Clear glass predominated, but blue, ruby, amber, and green were made in cut glass designs.

Breakfast castors often had egg cups and egg spoons and were limited to three or four bottles.

Castor handles could be purchased separately and were offered with call bells or vases included. Bottles also were a separate item featured in catalogs of the times.

Because of the value and desirability of Castor bottles to Art glass collectors, many became separated from the original frames. Now, with the value of Victorian Silverplate items increasing, complete castor sets with good intact cut or engraved bottles, especially those in color complete with tops, are bringing top prices.

CASTORS

*Retail
Silverplate
$40.00-$125.00
Silver
$100.00-$350.00

DINNER
CASTORS
CIRCA 1865

*Price Depends
On Number of
Bottles & Condition

Handsome 6 bottle dinner castor with deer head ornaments. Product of the Meriden Britannia Co. and made between 1885 and 1867. Height 18 inches.

CASTORS

*Retail
Silverplate
$40.00-$125.00
Silver
$100.00-$350.00

ALL
CIRCA
1880

CASTORS

GREEN'S
PATENT

REVOLVING
CASTOR

CIRCA
1860

VERY RARE

*Retail **$200.00**
*With Original Bottles in working condition.

CASTORS—PICKLE CASTORS

Closely related to Dinner & Breakfast Castors is this decorative and practical novelty item of 1870-1900.

The Pickle Castor consisted of a Silverplate frame with handle, tongs, or fork, and a round glass insert with a knob-top Silverplate cover.

Elaborate and fancy designs in pickle castors proliferated. Frames, handles, and tongs were coordinated with the same design theme repeated on all pieces.

The glass inserts were made of pressed, cut or engraved, or decorated glass. Most bottles were clear glass, but cut-glass in amber, blue, green and cranberry were available. Cut and molded glass bottles of Rubina Verde, Satin Glass, Amberina, Peachblow, Agata, etc. were made, and offered in catalogs of the 1880's as selections to be combined with castor frames.

Complete original castors with Cut Glass or Art Glass bottles are rare and quite valuable.

*Retail
All Made of Silverplate
Clear Or Pressed Glass: $50.00-$80.00
Art Glass; Amber, Blue, Red: $85.00-$250.00

CIRCA
1870

*Price Depends On Design & Glass Bottle

220

Clear Glass—$50.00-$80.00
Art Glass—$85.00-$200.00

2 Bottle
Set
Worth
More

FRUIT DISHES & STANDS

The early fruit stands of the 1860's featured pressed glass, or cut and engraved crystal on silver plated frames, and stands of simple beaded, gadrooned, or engraved designs.

By the mid 1870's, the fruit stand was the focal point of the dining table. The base and the glass bowl became more ornate and elaborate. Silver plate manufacturers vied with each other in creating fruit stands featuring floral motifs, cherubs, birds, fantastic animals, classic and mythological figures, and roccoco motifs on either a center pedestal or four low feet.

The glass bowls were made in many varieties of art glass: Agata, Amberina, Burmese, Satin, Malachite, Peachblow, clear, colored, etc., in pressed, cut, engraved, and etched were used.

Fruit stands are difficult to find complete with their glass containers, due to breakage and their desireability to art glass collectors.

Note: Reproductions are imported from foreign countries.

*Retail   Silver—$75.00-$200.00   Silverplate—$85.00-$150.00

"Tree of Life"
Pattern Bowl
CIRCA 1880

Cut
Crystal
Bowl

CIRCA
1875

FRUIT DISHES & STANDS

*Price Depends on Design,
Type of Glass Insert
Cut Crystal & Art Glass
Are Most Valuable

FRUIT DISH
CIRCA 1880

All are Made
Of Silverplate

FORKS

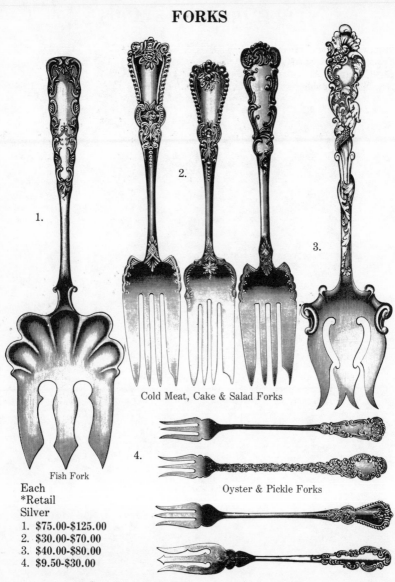

1.

2.

3.

Cold Meat, Cake & Salad Forks

4.

Oyster & Pickle Forks

Fish Fork

Each
*Retail
Silver

1. $75.00-$125.00
2. $30.00-$70.00
3. $40.00-$80.00
4. $9.50-$30.00

*NOTE: Silverplate Prices are 1/2 quotes prices.

FORKS

Forks as we know them today orignated in Italy during the early 1500's perhaps as a by-product of the Renaissance and the resurgence of cleanliness and manners of the period.

The fork was introduced to England in the 1600's as an eating utensil, prior to this forks were used only as serving pieces.

Until the early 1700's travelling forks were the rule and were carried along with a table knife by those who travelled.

In pre-Civil War America, simple table forks made of coin silver were used. These usually had four prongs and the typical "Fiddle Back" of the times. Like the coin silver spoons, the initials of the owner were often engraved on the handle, and the makers' hallmark was stamped on the underside of the stem.

American forks of the Victorian and Post-Civil War period (1865-1900) proliferated in a very large variety of designs and types. Featured in catalogs of silver manufacturers of the times were such items as; Fish Forks, Lettuce Forks, Ice Cream Forks, Tomato Forks, Cucumber Forks, Cold Meat Forks, Sardine Forks, Oyster and Pickle Forks, Berry Forks, Salad Forks, Etc.

Like the spoons of Victorian times the design and embellishments on serving and dining forks were in every style and fashion.

Classic, rococo, Romanesque, Floral, Art Nouveau designs appeared on handle, stems, and prongs. Prongs ranged from two prong berry forks, to six prong fish forks. Prongs were straight curved, or arrow shaped.

Individual large serving forks are rising in value and may be found in antique stores and flea markets.

Sets of 4, 6, 8, 12, 14, etc. in the same pattern are valuable particularly in sterling silver. Since most patterns were made in both sterling and silverplate, knowledge of the makers' hallmarks is important.

FORKS

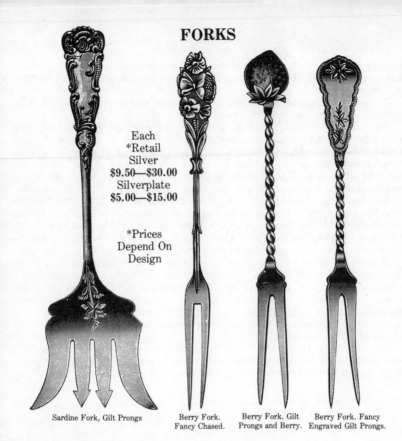

Each
*Retail
Silver
$9.50—$30.00
Silverplate
$5.00—$15.00

*Prices
Depend On
Design

Sardine Fork, Gilt Prongs

Berry Fork.
Fancy Chased.

Berry Fork. Gilt
Prongs and Berry.

Berry Fork. Fancy
Engraved Gilt Prongs.

Bread Fork

ART NOUVEAU

*SILVER—$75.00—$125.00

ICE WATER PITCHERS

Before the invention and proliferation of the mechanical refrigerator, the multi-wall insulated ice pitcher was a popular table device for serving cold water. The double and treble inner walls kept the ice from melting. The outer bodies were usually made of silverplate and were embossed, chased and engraved in designs and ornaments characteristic of the Victorian period. The ice pitcher had its heyday from 1860-1900.

Because of the weight of the pitcher (ten pounds and over) tilting devices were an improvement evolved in the 1870's. The stands, goblets (One or two), waste bowls, and handles were elaborately decorated in the same motif employed on the ice pitcher.

Original complete tilting water sets are quite valuable and difficult to find.

*Retail
Silverplate
$50.00-$125.00

†Silver
$200.00-$500.00

ICE WATER
PITCHER
CIRCA 1868

*Price Depends
On Size, Design
Condition

†Also Weight
Of Silver

ICE WATER PITCHERS
TILTING SETS

Tilting
Ice Water
Pitcher
CIRCA 1886

*Retail
Silverplate
$125.00—$200.00
†Silver
$250.00—$600.00

*Price Depends
On Design &
Condition

†Also Weight
Of Silver

ICE WATER PITCHERS
TILTING SETS

SILVERPLATED
TILTING WATER SETS
CIRCA 1890

*Each
Retail
Silverplate
$150.00-$300.00
†Silver
$300.00-$750.00

ICE TUBS AND WINE COOLERS

Wine coolers were made during the late 1700's, and were derived from the wine cisterns of the middle 1600's and early 1700's. Cisterns were elaborately embossed large oval bowls, chased with dolphins, mermaids, etc., designed to hold water, ice, and a quantity of wine bottles. They reached very large proportions in the 1700's, often four feet long, and over 1,000 ounces of sterling silver in weight.

Wine coolers which evolved from these cisterns, were made much smaller and more graceful, and held only one bottle of wine. They were usually vase shaped, either footed on a pedestal, or flat, with two handles. The interior was a removeable jacket which held the bottle; the ice was placed between the jacket and outside of the vase. Wine coolers were generally made in pairs, in silver and Sheffield plate in England, and in silver and silverplate in the United States. The designs often featured the grape and leaf motif, although the 1860's and 1900's saw the use of Victorian, rococo, and Art Nouveau designs engraved, inlaid and embossed.

*Silverplate—$60.00-$130.00
†Silver—$150.00-$350.00

Ice Tub

Wine Cooler

*Prices Depend on Size, Design &
†Weight of Silver

Ice Tub

KNIVES

The history of knives antedates that of forks, though knives with silver handles were not made before 1700. In earlier times in England, men carried a sheathed knife that was used both for defense and for eating. The introduction of silver handled table knives in the beginning of the eighteenth century ended the use of sheath knife at the dining table.

Many handle designs, pistol handle shape, reeded forms, plain forms, the shell motif, etc., originating in this period were later copied in the Victorian era, 1840 - 1900. Carving knives, and carving sets, bread knives and sets, were produced by all American silver and silverplate manufacturers in a variety of styles and types. Many had stag horn handles with silver pommels. Blades generally were of steel on these knives and when a silver or silverplate handle was used, the embellishment was rococo or floral in the Victorian fashion.

Desert knives, table knives, fruit knives, butter knives, etc., were made in the table-setting patterns of each manufacturer, the handles reflecting the rococo, Victorian, and Art Nouveau influences in etched, or embossed designs. Mother-of-Pearl or ivory were often combined with silver on the handles.

Matching sets of 4,6,8,12,14,24, etc., are collectable, valuable, and saleable. Individual place-setting knives are of less value.

*Silver†	*Silver†
1. $45.00-$125.00	2. $8.50-$15.00

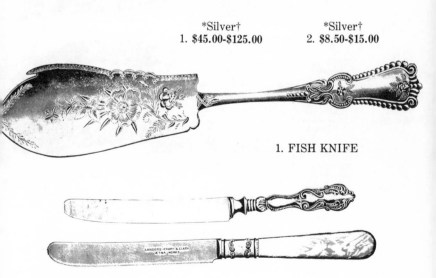

1. FISH KNIFE

2. TABLE KNIVES

*Price Depends on Design, Pattern, Weight.
†Note: Silverplate ½-Quoted Prices.

KNIVES
CARVING KNIVES & SETS

3 PIECE SET

Silver Trim
$60.00-$90.00

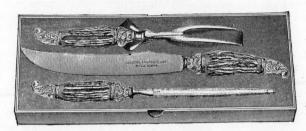

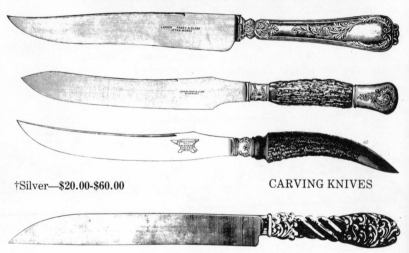

†Silver—$20.00-$60.00

CARVING KNIVES

BREAD KNIFE

FISH & ICE CREAM KNIVES

Triangular shaped and pierced sterling silver fish knives, or slices, were used in the middle 1700's. The asymmetrical shape fish slice had a single cutting edge, a curved pointed tip, and was made completely of silver.

The engraved designs on the blades of fish slices of the mid-1800's, generally had a fish motif as the subject. During the Victorian period the popular foliate scrolls and floral motifs appeared on the blades and handles. Ice cream knives, or slicers, were similar to fish slices, though smaller in size and less elaborately engraved.

JACK KNIVES—POCKET KNIVES

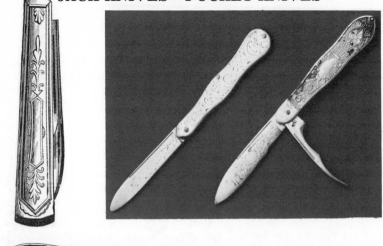

*Retail
Silverplate—$7.50-$35.00
Silver—$10.00-$50.00

*Price Depends on Size, Design,
Inlays, Ivory, Pearl Etc.

These charming, folding pocket knives were made by all silver and silverplate manufacturers: Rogers Bros., Gorham, Samuel Kirk, Unger Bros., etc., from 1860-1920.

They were advertised as "Fruit Knives" and usually had one curved blade with a single cutting edge. Often a "Nut Pick" blade accompanied the cutting blade. The "Nut Pick" was a slender curved bar used to extract the meat from the nut. Victorian designs were embossed, etched, or engraved on the body and handle of the pocket knife. Mother-of-Pearl, ivory, ebony, etc. were inlaid on sterling or silverplate on some models. Fruit Knives are growing rapidly in value and interest to collectors.

MATCH BOXES & SAFES

MATCH BOXES

These small boxes with hinged lids were made of many materials—pewter, copper, brass, tin, nickel-silver, Sterling Silver and Silverplate, as a carrying device for inflammable phosphorous matches before the days of lighters and safety matches. They were produced in a large variety of designs and shapes from 1890 to 1910. Manufacturers such as Gorham, Unger Bros., Reed & Barton, Elgin American, Samuel Kirk, Meriden Brittania, C. W. Sedgwick, W. B. Kerr, R. Blackinton & Co., Wm. A. Rogers, etc., made many boxes in Rococo, Oriental, and Art Nouveau decorations.

Sport subjects such as fishing, hunting, golfing, baseball, football, were popular, Animal designs abounded, and often the match box itself was in the shape of an animal. Historic, patriotic, and commemorative themes were depicted and used as souvenirs of special occasions. There are match boxes with romantic paintings reproduced in elaborate embossing and chasing depicting nudes, cupids and nymphs. Unger Brothers of Newark, N.J., produced many Art Nouveau subjects; fantastic Sea Serpents, Sea nymphs, dragons, nudes with flowing hair, noble Indians in full headdress, covered the Sterling Silver surface.

Figural boxes in the shape of a boot or shoe, a hat, a bale of cotton, a basket, an elephant's head, a horse's head, a swaddling baby, a pig, a cat, a monkey, an owl, a violin, Columbus head, a valise, etc. all are very desirable and collectable. Advertising match boxes are usually plated and carry an inscribed sales message.

Art Nouveau, Advertising, and Figural Boxes are the most sought-after at this time, and are the most valuable.

*Retail
Silverplate—$8.50-$35.00
Sterling Silver—$12.00-$85.00

*Price Depends on Design, Size.

Advertising Art Nouveau, Repousse, Figurals are the most valuable.

MATCH BOXES & MATCH SAFES

All Prices are for Sterling Silver
Silverplate—1/2 Prices Quoted.

$15-$25.00 $12-$25.00 $15-$30.00 $10-$20.00

$12-$25.00 $10-$20.00 $30-$50.00   BACK

$10-$20.00 $10-$20.00 $15-$30.00 $30-$50.00 $10-$20.00

$30-$60.00 $40.00 $10-$20.00 $10-$20.00 $20-$40.00

235

MATCH SAFES &
TOOTHPICK HOLDERS

Here is an instance where the same practical product was used for a dual function, for dispensing either toothpicks or wooden matches.

A variety of human and animal motifs were the subjects of these table-top receptacles. Silver plated dogs, birds, chicks, bears, frogs and monkeys, deported themselves along with the container holding either matches or toothpicks.

Cherubs, angels, and playful kiddies held or carried the match or toothpick receptacle.

*Retail Silverplate—$50.00-$150.00

*Price Depends on Design & Condition.

NAPKIN RINGS

A true product of the Victorian era introduced to the American public circa 1860, the napkin ring was produced by all Silver & Silverplate manufacturers including: The Meriden Britannia Company, Meriden Silver Plate Company, Reed & Barton, Pairpont Manufacturing Company, Derby Silver Company, Homan Manufacturing Company, Aurora Silver Plate Company, Acme Silver Company, Rockford Silver Plate Company, and many others.

By the 1870's hundreds of varieties and designs had appeared, the earlier simple rings in silver and silverplate decorated with engraving, engine turning, beading, piercing, and applied medallions. The origin of the figural napkin rings was as a training device for Victorian children, to encourage them to roll up their napkins and insert them in the rings. The Victorian penchant for whimsy asserted itself in these items with a veritable menagerie of animals: cats, dogs, chickens, rabbits, squirrels, goats and ponies pulling wheeled carts holding rings, turtles carrying rings on their backs, birds, butterflies, and others disporting themselves. Cherubs and playing children were also a popular motif for figural rings.

Combination caster sets with pepper shaker, salt dish and napkin ring, usually with a cherub or some other figure are valuable.

All types of figural napkin rings are very popular with collectors and dealers.

Possibly as a result of their popularity, reproductions of figural napkins are imported and sold in the U.S.

*Retail
Silverplate
$7.50-$80.00
Silver
$25.00-$100.00

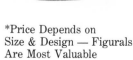

*Price Depends on
Size & Design — Figurals
Are Most Valuable

NAPKIN RINGS

FIGURALS
Silverplate
$50.00-$200.00

CIRCA 1870

NAPKIN
RING
SET
$180.00

Silverplate
FIGURAL
$150.00

NUT BOWLS

The nut bowl is an example of art (and artisans) imitating nature. These vessels were often made in the shape of an acorn, walnut, coconut, etc., embellished with oak leaves, dragon flies, acorns, etc., and often featuring a "bright-eyed and bushy-tailed" squirrel on the rim or base. They were made by Wm. Rogers Mfg. Co., Wilcox Silver Plate Co., Derby Silver, Simpson, Hall, Miller & Co., etc. Circa 1880's - 1900's.

*Retail
Silverplate
$30.00-$125.00
†Silver
$50.00-$200.00

NUT BOWL
Silverplate
CIRCA 1880

"SEA SHELL"
NUT BOWL
CIRCA 1888

*Price Depends on Design, Size, Glass Insert.
†Weight of Silver

NUT BOWLS

SEE PAGE 239 FOR
ALL RETAIL PRICES

"FILIGREE"
NUT BOWL
CIRCA 1890

"SQUIRREL"
NUT BOWL
CIRCA 1890

"VENETIAN" NUT BOWL
CIRCA 1887

PITCHERS

Water pitchers were a popular item of Silver & Silverplate production from 1860 - 1910. The common water pitcher had no covers, unlike the double and triple wall Ice-Water Pitchers. They were also made in sets with a tray and two or three matching cups.

Elaborate designs covered the surface and handle, chased, engraved, engine turned, and embossed. The Art Noveau period resulted in a proliferation of sinuous designs of nudes, mermaids, fish, waves, flowers, exotic animals, etc., often with matching trays.

Sterling Silver and Martelé pitchers are very desirable and valuable.

*Retail
Silverplate—$25.00-$80.00
†Silver—$150.00-$300.00

*Price Depends on
Design, Size, Condition
†& Weight of
Silver

"CROCUS" PATTERN
WATER PITCHER
CIRCA 1904

Most valuable are Art Nouveau designs

PITCHERS

SEE
PG. 241
FOR PRICES

MARTELÉ
PITCHER
ART
NOUVEAU

"FERN" DESIGN
CIRCA 1900

WATER SET—SILVER
PITCHER, GOBLET, TRAY

Retail—$250.00

Fern design water pitcher. Meriden Britannia Co. catalog, no date.
Marked "Discontinued Jan. 1907."

SYRUP PITCHERS

Syrup pitchers were functional table items for dispensing maple syrup or other liquid toppings, produced from the 1860's-1910. The early ones were sold with a small drip plate, eliminated in later models, containing a built-in cut-off. They were made in a large variety of designs sometimes matching a tea or coffee set.

SYRUP
PITCHER
& DRIP
PLATE
CIRCA
1870

PORRINGERS

These table items were made in great quantities in the 1600's and 1700's in both England and the American Colonies. The porringer was a circular shallow bowl with a decorative handle usually pierced.

Silver & Silverplate porringers were made in the 1800's but not in great quantities. Martelé Sterling Silver porringers made by Gorham in Art Nouveau designs are the most valuable of the 1800's.

PUNCH BOWLS AND LADLES

The ceremonial punch bowl and set was an important part of festivities in Georgian England. From the 1860's through the 1890's it was also made by all silver and silverplate producers. The set consisted of punch bowl, tray, cups and ladle. The designs on silverplate usually centered around the grape and leaf motif.

American Sterling silver punch bowls were generally made on assignment for a commemorative occasion or the launching of a warship. So called "American Navy Presentation Silver," was donated to the warship by the citizens of the city or state after which the warship was named.

The Martelé silver pieces were one-of-a-kind examples of the silversmith's art made only by the Gorham Company. They featured Art Nouveau motifs, embossed and chased. Sea serpents, mermaids sporting in the waves, King Neptune and sea nymphs, floral and leaf motifs, satyr and nymphs covered the surface of bowl, ladle, cups and bases. Of the punch bowl pieces made in the period 1860's-1910 by American manufacturers, the Martelé examples are the most valuable.

PUNCH BOWL, CUPS & LADLE
CIRCA 1895

Retail
Silverplate—$500.00

PUNCH BOWLS & LADLES

MARTELE PUNCH SET, BOWL, LADLES, CUPS, TRAY

*Sterling Silver—$7500.00

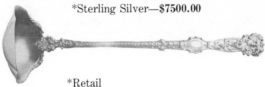

*Retail
Silverplate
$20.00-$60.00
Silver
$75.00-$200.00

PUNCH LADLES

*Prices Depend on Size, Design,& Weight of Silver

SALT CELLAR & SALT SHAKERS

At the end of the 1600's small "trencher salts" came into popular use as vessels for dispensing salt at the individual plate or "trencher." These small salts replaced the "great salt" that was the centerpiece of Middle Ages dining tables.

The early salts of the American variety were usually round, about three inches in diameter, and set on low pedestals or legs. They were decorated in the Victorian fashion with gadrooned edges, beading, chasing, and surface engraving and engine turning. The popular "lion mask" often appeared in miniature over each foot. Gilt linings or ruby glass inserts were the rule in these items. During the 1870's salts were made in diverse shapes, small round bowls and tubs with cast animal figures and other motifs. The fluted shell shape was a popular theme, and Silverplate frames in a large variety of designs with handles, and sometimes spoons, graced the tables of the period.

These open slat dishes had inserts of clear, frosted, ruby or colored glass which were often pressed or engraved.

The "Shaker Salt" (or Salt-Shaker) came into general use in the late 1870's aided by inventions and devices that prevented the salt from caking and the "Shakers" from corroding. The Victorian penchant for whimsy in small practical items asserted itself. Meriden, Brittania, Rogers Bros., Reed & Barton, Wilcox Silver, and others blossomed forth with a menagerie of cats, owls, dogs (in and out of barrels), parrots, chickens, rabbits, little Miss with Muff, little Mister with top hat, miniature champagne bottles ("Extra Dry Pepper"), and conventional shapes galore. These items were often advertised as "Peppers" since open salts were still made and used, although later catalogues defined them as "Peppers and Salts."

The "Pepper & Salt" castor sets were set on a low footed heavily decorated Silverplate frame with a center carrying handle to "pass the salt" at table. The shakers were of cut, pressed, engraved, or enamelled glass embellished with typical Victorian designs, flowers, scenery, birds, and Rococo elaborate curlicues. The pierced shaker tops were either Sterling or Silverplate.

As a group these Salt and Salt & Pepper Shakers are very collectable and desired by dealers and the public.

SALT CELLAR & SALT SHAKER

Silverplate—$7.50-$30.00 Each
Sterling Silver—$10.00-$60.00 Each

SALTS & SPOONS

SALT CELLAR

*Silver—$40.00Each

*Silver—$50.00Each

*Silver
$30.00

PEPPER AND SALT

*Silver
$60.00

*Silverplate — ½-Prices Quoted

247

SPOONS

As a group of silver and silverplate collectables, spoons offer the greatest assortment of styles, types, designs, and forms. The Victorian and Art Nouveau periods (1840-1910) saw the creation of a large variety of spoons for every conceivable table use. Aside from the table setting spoons, they were made as Berry spoons, Ice Cream spoons, Jelly spoons, Bonbon spoons, olive spoons, salad spoons, sugar shells, sugar sifter, pea spoons, coffee spoons, Vienna coffee spoons, Apostle spoons, souvenir spoons, etc. Books have been written on the subject of spoons, and individual categories of spoons such as: AMERICAN SPOONS, SOUVENIR AND HISTORICAL by Dorothy T. Rainwater. For anyone interested in spoons these types of books are highly recommended.

The handles of spoons of all types were the object of much design and decoration. Hundreds of designs were created by the largest silverware producers, many being made in both sterling and plate. They ran the style gamut; rococo, baroque, romanesque, Victorian themes, flowers of every type, human figures such as the "Nuremberg" coffee spoons decorated with peasants and noblemen in costumes of Old Nuremberg.

Every silver production technique was used in the manufacture of spoons; embossing, casting, repousse, chasing, engraving, etching, etc. Coffee spoons, Apostle spoons, and souvenir spoons reached the height of intricate designs and figures. Beautiful enameling, gilding, and inlay work were also used extensively on coffee and souvenir spoons.

The bowls of table setting spoons were usually plain and oval in shape. Berry and salad spoons, bonbon spoons, olive spoons, sugar sifters, etc. all had elaborate piercing and cutout patterns, and scalloped and irregular edges. Stems of these spoons and coffee and souvenir spoons were often twisted and embellished.

Comic character spoons of the 1930's and 1940's with engraved or embossed figures of: Mickey Mouse, Howdy Doody, Charlie McCarthy, etc., are a popular category of silver spoons growing in value.

Complete sets of spoons, 6, 8, 12, 14, 24, etc. are much more valuable than individual items or mixed patterns.

Coin silver spoons made from melted down silver coins were extensively made in pre-1860 America by individual silversmiths. Coin silver spoons are light in weight, bowls are "egg shape," handles are usually "fiddle shape" with the owners' name or initials engraved thereon. Makers' hallmarks are stamped on the underside of the handles. Complete sets are rising in value.

SPOONS

COIN SILVER SPOONS — ROGERS BROS. 1825-61

Retail
$10.00-$15.00 Each
Set of 6
$85.00

ROGERS BROS. SILVERPLATED SPOON — 1847

SPOONS

SUGAR SHELL
$12.50-$25.00

COMIC
CHARACTER
SPOON

SALAD
SPOON
$30.00-$80.00

BERRY
OR SALAD
SPOON
$15.00-$30.00

BON-BON &
JELLY SPOONS
$15.00-$30.00

"LA VIGNE"
PATTERN
ROGERS
BROS. 1881
$6.50
to
$15.00

COFFEE or SOUVENIR SPOON
$10.00 - $25.00

Silverplate—1/2 Quoted Prices

SPOON HOLDERS—SPOON RACKS

Unlike the Spoon Warmer, the Spoon Holder is exclusively an American development. The two handled "Vase" shaped holder, circa 1860, stood on low pedestals and resembled miniature "Loving Cups" with restrained ornamentation. By the 1870's, Victorian ostentation in design appeared on the spoon holders.

Elaborate embossing, engraving, repousse and chasing, and classic medallions and lions heads were common as motifs.

Double spoon holders were made by most American Silverplate producers of the 1870's and 1880's. Elaborate embellished stands with castor type bail handles, some with bells or vases, held the two compartments into which the spoons were inserted.

In the mid 1870's the combination sugar bowl and spoon rack evolved. The racks on the rim of the bowl held six or twelve spoons, the sugar bowls stood on a pedestal with the cover usually crowned in a decorative finial—a bird, animal, or butterfly figural.

Spoon holders were often decorated in a matching pattern to the tea and coffee sets of the 1880's.

RETAIL

$20.00 - $40.00*

*$35.00 to $50.00

$10.00 - $25.00

*Prices Do Not Include Spoons

TEAPOTS, TEAKETTLES, & SETS

The ceremony of tea drinking in England and on the Continent was of such importance to the nobles and the wealthy that the finest silversmiths produced beautiful examples of teapots, teakettles, and tea sets throughout the ages. If any one item can be said to represent the height of the silversmith's art, it is the teapot and teakettle and its companion pieces the sugar and creamer.

Designs of teapots and sets ranged through all periods and influences: Medieval, Renaissance, Classic, Baroque, Rococo, Queen Anne, Georgian (George I, II, III, IV) are all represented. Shapes were as varied as the designs; round, oval, octagonal, oblong, bullet-shaped, pear-shaped, inverted pear-shape, baluster shape, pumpkin-shaped, etc.

Every type of surface, decoration, casting, molding, engraving, chasing, repoussé, gadrooning, beading was employed. Tea kettles were generally globular in shape with an attached swing handle, usually on matching stand. They followed the style and design of teapots. Footed stands containing a warming lamp are found with both teakettles and teapots.

Tea pot handles were usually "S" or "C" shaped wood or silver handles attached to the body.

American teapots, teakettles and sets were made by all silver companies during the Victorian and Art Nouveau periods 1840-1910. The main design influence on Victorian items was elaborate rococo and featured repousse over-all naturalistic decorative patterns of elaborate floral detail, often combined with engraved or chased scenes of sweetness and sentiment. Curved shapes were the most popular for bodies, handles, legs and spouts. Combinations of styles were used on many Victorian pieces of silver and silverplate during the decades of 1870-1900. Designs mixing elements of Renaissance and Elizabethan, Oriental and Rococo Classic and Japanese, are often found on the same teapot and tea sets; this mixed style is also known as "Eclectic."

The Victorian and Art Nouveau Sterling Silver and Silverplate pieces are increasing in value rapidly. Complete sets with teapot, teakettle, creamer, sugar, and waste bowl are most sought after.

TEAPOTS, TEAKETTLES & SETS

VICTORIAN TEAPOT
CIRCA 1877

*Retail
Silverplate
$40.00-$175.00

VICTORIAN
TEA POT
CIRCA 1872

TEAPOTS
*Sterling Silver
$80.00-$350.00

*Prices Based on Design, Condition, Weight of Silver

TEAPOTS, TEAKETTLES & SETS

*Silver
$75.00 - $200.00

*Silverplate —
½-Prices Quoted

TEA KETTLE
CIRCA 1888

TEAPOT
CIRCA 1867

*Silver
$350.00 - $600.00

TEA KETTLE
CIRCA 1878

*Silver
$200 - $350

*Price
Depends on
Condition &
Weight of Silver

TEA & COFFEE SETS

*Retail Silverplate $300.00-$850.00 †Silver $1800.00-$2250.00 CIRCA 1867

†Price Depends on Design & Weight of Silver

*Retail Silverplate $40.00-$90.00 †Silver $200.00-$500.00

*Price Depends on Condition & Design of Silver

TEA & COFFEE SETS

CIRCA
1905

MARTELÉ
*Retail
Silver
$4500.00

*Retail†
"CHARTER OAK" SILVERWARE
$250.00 - $450.00

†Silver 6-Piece Set Double Priced Depending on Condition

TEA SETS

*Retail
Silverplate
$250.00-$400.00
†Silver
$2500.00-$3500.00

CIRCA
1877

*Retail
Silverplate
$200.00-$350.00
†Silver
$650.00-$1250.00

TANKARDS, MUGS, CUPS, & GOBLETS

Tankards of Sterling Silver were an important drinking vessel of the 1600's and 1700's usually made with a plain cylindrical body and a flat projecting rim. The hinged cover had a decorated thumb-grip to enable the cover to be opened and closed. Tankards usually had an "S" shaped handle. They were made throughout the 1800's, to early 1900's and followed the traditional form and designs.

MUGS & CANNS

The Mug was derived from the Tankard, being slightly smaller without a cover and mainly used for drinking beer. Canns were similar to mugs differing only in being slightly larger. Form and design followed Tankards very closely.

GOBLETS

Goblets were widely used during the 1600's. In effect, they were flat or curved bottomed cups set on a single foot with a round base. Goblets and cups in the 1860's-1900 were made in a large variety of styles and were engraved, chased, embossed and decorated with medallions, swags, floral motifs, engine turning, etc. Art Nouveau pieces in silver have risen rapidly in price in the past years.

CHILDREN'S CUPS

Children's cups were embellished with subjects such as: Nursery Rhymes, Clowns, Birds, Flowers, Animals, etc. They were produced in hundreds of varieties by American silver manufacturers.

SPECIAL CUPS

Shaving cups, or mugs, are described and priced under "Gentlemens' Items." Mustache cups made of Silver & Silverplate were equipped with a guard inside the cup that kept the 1880's gentleman's mustache from dipping into the coffee or tea.

The cups and matching saucers were often elaborately engraved and these sets are the most valuable.

TANKARDS, MUGS, CUPS

*Silver
$25.00-$75.00

ART
NOUVEAU
CIRCA
1905

*Silver
$30.00-$90.00

*Retail
Silver—$100.00-$350.00

CIRCA
1895

MUSTACHE CUP
& SAUCER

*Silver
$25.00-$75.00

*Price Depends on Size, Design & Weight of Silver.
Silverplate — ½-Price Quoted

TOBACCO ITEMS

SMOKING SETS, ASH TRAYS, CIGAR AND TOBACCO BOXES

The use of tobacco and its by products, cigarettes, cigars, pipes, etc. were the basis of many collectable and interesting Silver & Silverplate items manufactured during the period 1860-1910. They were produced in a large variety of types and designs: Victorian, Rococco, Art Nouveau, etc., embossed, chased or engraved. Cigar boxes were hinged or covered, oblong or square shaped, with cast figures (often pipes) or handles on top.

SMOKER'S SETS

Consisted of cigar or cigarette receptacle, match holder, and ash tray on a matching tray, complete sets are difficult to find. They were made in both silver & silverplate in a large variety of Victorian & Art Nouveau designs.

ASH TRAYS

Often the practical feature of a cigar or match holder was combined with the ash tray. Borders were heavily embellished and cast metal cigars or pipes were frequently used as rests. Engraved humorous themes and mottos were common.

Art Nouveau ash trays in Sterling Silver, made by Unger Bros. Silversmiths of Newark, N.J., featured sensuous nudes, and ladies with flowing hair, cherubs, full face Indian Chief in headdress, smoking man, etc. These are quite rare and valuable.

CIGAR & CIGARETTE CASES

After 1900 the use of "ready-made" cigarettes proliferated. Cases to carry both cigarettes and cigars were made by many Silver & Silverplate manufacturers. Single row and double row cases were produced for cigarettes in a large variety of Art Nouveau and Rococco designs, and in the 1920's and 30's in Art Deco motifs. Cigar cases were made in the same styles and designs although they are considerably larger. Sterling Silver, Unger Bros. cases decorated in Art Nouveau motifs are most valuable and desirable.

TOBACCO ITEMS
ASH TRAYS

*Retail
Silver
$60.00-$150.00
Each

Silverplate
$30.00-$75.00

CIGAR &
CIGARETTE
BOXES

CIGAR LAMP
*Silver
$25.00-$65.00

*Retail
Silver
$60.00-$200.00 Each
Silverplate
$40.00-$150.00

SMOKING
SET

Silverplate—$25.00-$80.00   Silver—$40.00-$150.00
*Price Depends on Design, Size & Weight of Silver

WAITERS, TRAYS AND SALVERS

The waiter and salver were trays used to serve tea, coffee, punch, etc. Shapes in Silver and Silverplate were generally oval, but also were made round, square, rectangular. During the Art Nouveau period shapes were eratic and irregular. Waiters shaped to curve around the body when carried were used in the 1870's. The borders were the focus of design and embellishments with beading, gadrooning, egg and tongue, rococco motifs, piercing, engraving, chasing, and repousse work. Center surface ornamentation, when used, was chasing or engraving with the designs often matching those on other items used in serving. Special purpose trays include bread trays, sandwich trays, crumb trays, children's trays, pin and trinket trays, etc.

Art Nouveau trays by Unger Brothers, and Martelé trays made by Gorham in Sterling Silver embellished with naturalistic floral motifs, flowing hair ladies, exotic fish and mermaids, are very desirable and valuable.

VICTORIAN
CIRCA
1870

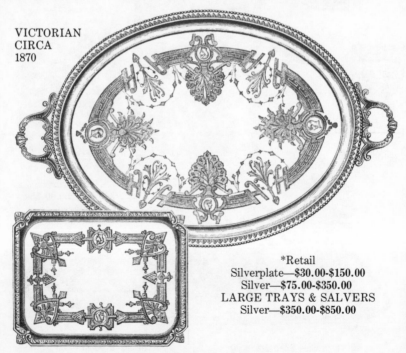

*Retail
Silverplate—$30.00-$150.00
Silver—$75.00-$350.00
LARGE TRAYS & SALVERS
Silver—$350.00-$850.00

*Price Depends on Size, Design & Weight of Silver.

Official Guide to Bottles
Old & New

By Hal L. Cohen

The most complete price guide and bottle book available. The book is divided into two parts, **Part 1:** Old collectable bottles—Whiskeys, Bitters, Inks, Milk Bottles, Flasks of all types, Medicine & Pharmacy, Beer & Coca Cola, Food Bottles, Perfume, Fruit Jars, Barber Bottles, Candy Containers, etc. listed, illustrated and priced. **Part 2:** New collectable bottles—Jim Beams'. Avon, Luxardo, Ezra Brooks, Lionstone, Wheaton, Garnier, The Grenadiers, Grant, Schenley, J. W. Dant, Jack Daniels, etc. listed, illustrated and priced. Also—History and information, grading, where to buy and sell, bottle clubs and publications.

Fully Illustrated 320 Pages 16 Color Pages 5x7
#154—$5.00

Official Guide to Comic
Books—The Price to
Buy & Sell

By Hal L. Cohen

This comprehensive book with over 200 illustrations covers the subject of Collectable Comic Books, and other related Collectables of all types from 1895 thru today. This book was prepared in consultation with Ed Summers (Supersnipe) one of the foremost authorities on comic collectibles in the U.S. From the earliest examples of American printed Comic Books such as "THE YELLOW KID" and "BUSTER BROWN" circa 1908, through "THE GOLDEN ERA" 1936-1960, thousands of Comic Books are listed alphabetically, by title, starting with "A-1 COMICS-1947," through "ZORRO 1965-67." The publsihers name and the "ISSUE NUMBERS" are listed, dated and priced in Fine & Mint Condition. A Value Scale is included to cover all issues in FAIR and GOOD. 224 pages, 5 x 7, 8 pages color. Also includes BIG LITTLE BOOKS.
329—$5.00

17 Park Avenue, New York, N.Y. 1001

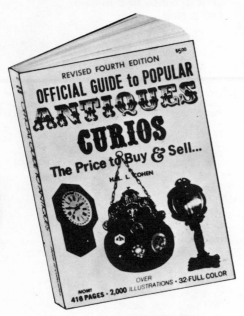